State of the Heart

STATE
of the
HEART

Stories of a
Humanitarian Israel

David Kramer

URIM PUBLICATIONS
Jerusalem • New York

Typeset by Ariel Walden
Printed in Israel
First Edition
ISBN 978-965-524-333-8
Urim Publications
P.O. Box 52287,
Jerusalem 9152102 Israel
www.UrimPublications.com

Library of Congress Cataloging-in-Publication Data

Names: Kramer, David, author.
Title: State of the heart : stories of a humanitarian Israel / David Kramer.
Description: First edition. | Jerusalem ; New York : Urim Publications, [2019]
Identifiers: LCCN 2019017155 | ISBN 9789655243338 (hardcover : alk. paper)
Subjects: LCSH: Humanitarian assistance, Israeli—History. | Israel—Foreign
    relations.
Classification: LCC HV555.I77 K73 2019 | DDC 361.6095694—dc23
LC record available at https://lccn.loc.gov/2019017155

Our parents, OSKAR and HENA OLINER, of blessed memory, and SHIMON and MARGIE SUMNER, of blessed memory, were devout and righteous Jews. They led exemplary lives of meticulous observance of ritual with generous displays of Chessed and Tzedokah, with an honest and wholesome lifestyle.

The Oliner door was always open to family and friends. The kitchen counter held HENA's famous sponge cake that was happily offered to everyone who graced their home. Sunday night dinners were a constant stream of honored guests who traveled from far and near to delight in scrumptious stuffed cabbage, brisket, and heavenly desserts. OSKAR, with his twinkling eyes and deadpan expression, could bring anyone to tears of laughter.

Shimmy and Margie were loved by all. SHIMMY had the widest smile and the biggest heart. His humor, countless jokes, and dancing feet were pure sunshine. MARGIE's list of friends was endless. Her engaging personality and uncanny ability to always push the right buttons was magnetic. Her daily phone calls are still sorely missed.

Our parents were diligent in their performance of Mitzvos to Hashem and Mitzvos to their neighbors. They would be proud to be associated with this fascinating story of human decency.

REVA & MARTY OLINER

Lawrence, NY

2019

"We do not rejoice in victories.
We rejoice when a new kind of
cotton is grown and when
strawberries bloom in
Israel."
– Golda Meir

Dedicated in Memory of Eyal Banin, *z"l*

(Photo credit: Arie Tennbaum, Pikiwiki Israel

Contents

Introduction

There is much that can be written that personifies the compassionate and humanitarian side of Israel and its people. A brief look at Jewish history chronicles the infinite struggles and challenges the Jewish people have faced over thousands of years of exile, and portrays our efforts to return to our Biblical and ancestral homeland. These experiences have been etched into the collective consciousness of the Jewish nation and reverberate in our behavior to this day. Stop an elderly person in the streets, in Jerusalem, Tel-Aviv, Haifa or anywhere in the country, and you are likely to hear an epic personal journey of how he/she arrived in Israel or about how they participated in one of the many wars or contributed in other ways to the building of the newly established country, some of which would certainly make for classic Hollywood films.

There is an old-age home across the street from where I live in Jerusalem. When speaking with any one of the residents it is difficult to avoid noticing the numbers tattooed on his or her arm, an emotional reminder of what the Nazis inflicted on Jews during the Holocaust. My home is in a multi-unit building and my neighbors on one side are from Libya, having been persecuted from their home country by the Libyan government. My neighbor on the other side is an immigrant from Morocco, whose family fled his hometown of Fez without any of their belongings following Israel's defeat of the Pan-Arab armies in 1948. These Jewish refugees, thrown out of their homes and homelands, could easily have succumbed to despair. Instead, they persevered in their new land and built a better life for themselves and their future generations.

Author's Note

The purpose of this book is not to portray Israel as a perfect country. I did not seek to over-simplify or ignore the myriad of complexities and issues facing Israeli society. Nor does it attempt to explain or delve into the many contributing factors behind the Israeli-Palestinian conflict. There are many other books for that. STATE OF THE HEART is rather a book about people and a look at the motivations, influences and philosophies that drive them to take action for the betterment of their immediate and global surroundings. For the sake of brevity and clarity, this collection of stories represents only a sampling of individuals and organizations who have gone above and beyond in their humanitarian efforts. There are so many others that deserve to be included and weren't. The majority of people, events and organizations included are ones I have been directly associated with and have come to know intimately. Thus for me, this book is also a personal journey. The book has been written in short-story format, so that each story stands on its own and within the context of the bigger picture.

My Story

In September 2000, I joined six Israeli students as a participant at the United Nations World Conference against Racism in Durban, South Africa. The purpose of our presence at the event was to take

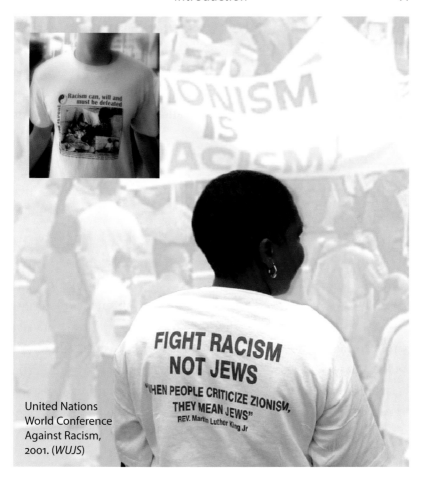

United Nations
World Conference
Against Racism,
2001. (*WUJS*)

part in a number of discussions and plenary sessions on issues
of anti-Semitism, the Holocaust, Israel and other global human
rights issues. Having been raised in South Africa, I was quite ex-
cited to attend this conference, especially to visit the coastal city of
Durban, a place which evoked many of my childhood memories.
There were rumors that Israel was going to be a topical issue at the
conference, however not one of us anticipated how events would
unfold. Upon arriving at the conference hall, I joined the long
line of participants at the registration desk and after filling out the
necessary forms, I noticed someone handing out free t-shirts at a

nearby table and I took one. I was shocked at what I saw. The shirt, printed with the official logo of the United Nations Conference against Racism, had the picture of Muhammed al-Dura and his father. They were two Palestinians, who were allegedly caught in a cross-fire between Palestinian gunmen and Israeli soldiers at the outbreak of the second Intifada in Israel several months earlier. I knew that the Israeli Defense Force had just released its findings on the incident, together with forensic diagrams made public in the news, which concluded that it was impossible that the two innocent bystanders were shot by Israeli soldiers. (This was later confirmed by several international investigations in the years following the event.) In Durban at the time, the truth did not matter to the thousands of people who were attending from all over the world and who paid scant attention to the wording and details of their free shirt. I attended the opening ceremony and once again, I was stunned with what I encountered. There, in Kingsmead Cricket stadium, a major-league baseball-style sports arena, 20,000 plus people were packed into the designated ceremony area, all wearing their white Muhammed al-Dura t-shirts, standing in unison against the State of Israel. By now, I had joined another Israeli participant, Ora, a young Israeli-Ethiopian student, who stood next to me as we took in the outrageous spectacle. In addition to the t-shirts, the stadium was covered in banners with the following accusations: "Zionism=Racism;" "Israel is an Apartheid State," and others equating Israel with Nazism. The events of the week continued along the same lines. Our delegation of six students together with the other representatives from Israel were assigned a full security detail that escorted us wherever we went. We were confronted daily by hundreds of protestors who threateningly approached our tent to shout us down and try to remove the Israeli flag. They shoved vile posters in our faces with all sorts of false accusations against Israel, and handed

United Nations World Conference Against Racism, 2001. (*WUJS*)

out anti-Semitic flyers, books and cartoons with Hitler's face star-
ing out at us from the cover. At the student conference, we tried
to pass a resolution calling for the end of violence on all sides of
the Israeli-Palestinian conflict and once again, to our astonishment, our efforts proved ineffective and the proposal was voted
down. We walked out of the meeting and did not return. At one
point during the conference, we decided to design and distribute
our own t-shirt and through a local sponsor we were able to produce thousands of shirts in record time. Our shirt had a blue Star
of David on the front with a peace sign in the middle and a quote
on the back from Martin Luther King Junior: "When people crit-
icize Zionism, they mean Jews." I ended up going on my own to
fetch the shirts from a nearby supplier, riding in a huge delivery
truck with a driver who had no idea of the purpose of the journey. When we arrived at the factory we loaded the large assort-
ment of shirts into the truck, and in order to save time, I rode in
the back of the windowless vehicle and began sorting the bags of
shirts according to sizes, as we had agreed to start handing out

the shirts as soon as the truck arrived at the conference. I was unable to see what was happening outside the truck, and the driver made no mention to me that making its way alongside the road toward the conference was one of the largest anti-Israel rallies that had ever taken place since Israel's establishment. I found out later that there were over 300,000 people marching together, chanting slogans against Israel and carrying banners with the same anti-Israel slogans used at the opening ceremony. I arrived safely at the conference's entrance and as a group, we immediately began to distribute our shirts. A few moments later, the anti-Israel rally arrived at the bend of the street close to where we were standing and one of the rally's organizers directed her followers to, "Stop the Israelis from handing out their shirts." We were immediately accosted and violently assaulted by the large crowd, and were only saved by the South African police who formed a protective circle around us. The next day, Mary Robinson, the deputy head of the United Nations at the time, invited our group on to the stage in front of the conference and apologized to us in person.

I chose the name STATE OF THE HEART for this book for two reasons. The first was to draw attention to the vast contrast and disconnect that exists in the general perception of Israel throughout the world today, especially in various councils, bodies and conferences of the United Nations. In several polls taken over the last few years, many people perceive that the biggest obstacle to world peace was, and still is, Israel. There have been more United Nations resolutions condemning Israel – sixty-two to date – than against all other countries in the world combined, and it is considered and treated worse in the international arena than many well-documented human rights abusers such as Iran, Syria, Saudi Arabia, South Sudan, North Korea, China, and Russia. In fact, during the writing of this book, the North Korean dictator, Kim Jong Un, had his defense chief executed for falling asleep during a meeting. Over 500,000 Syrians have been killed and approximately 1.2 million displaced as a result of the ongoing civil war in their country – a war initiated by their own government and facilitated with Iranian and Russian support. At the same time, over 1,000 people were sentenced to death without trial in Saudi Arabia, Kuwait, Bahrain and Sudan while many other human rights atrocities have been overlooked. Israel is subjected to a global boycott, sanctions and divestment movement against it, which continues unabated throughout parts of the world today, including on college and university campuses, in the United States and elsewhere. The reality in Israel is, however, the opposite of how we are understood. As the pages of STATE OF THE HEART reveal, Israel and its citizens, amidst all the challenges, display an uncompromising desire for the welfare, protection and advancement of all human life, in Israel, the Middle East and throughout the world. The State of Israel might be a tiny country, but it's a nation with a big heart and its humanitarian imprint can be felt in almost every corner of the earth.

The second reason for choosing the name STATE OF THE HEART, came to me precipitously while I was writing the book. The more I immersed myself in the narratives of the book, the more I sensed that the people and stories featured throughout the book provide the reader with inspiring life examples that can expand and enhance one's own personal outlook and the world at large. I felt the book had the potential to provide the reader with a deeper personal message that went beyond Israel, and I envisioned it serving as a catalyst to enable one to explore issues such as: appreciation for life; compassion toward others; reaching out to people we disagree with; helping the less fortunate; turning tragedy into opportunities for growth; applying technology for good, and more. We are living in a disenfranchised world, where changing political and global landscapes coupled with the centrality of social and political media in our lives have created a situation where healthy debate and tolerance of varying and conflicting opinions and ideas become challenging undertakings. Therefore, it is my sincere hope that this book serves to enable an honest discourse on issues of humanity, tolerance, unity and understanding – and the examination of our own personal *state of the heart* toward ourselves and the world around us.

Despite all the societal issues, political complexities and regional complications, Israel is a free, benevolent and peace-seeking nation. Even following the wave of Palestinian stabbing and car-ramming attacks against Israelis, starting in 2014, the annual peace index survey conducted by The Israeli Democracy Institute and Tel Aviv University found that 60% of Israeli Jews polled continued to believe that conducting peace negotiations with the Palestinian Authority was the best way to go, even though they did not necessarily feel this would lead to peace.

In 2015, Israel was ranked by the OECD as one of the top five "happiest" countries in the world. A follow-up article in the Asian Times put it this way: "Israel is the happiest nation on earth. . . . It is one of the wealthiest, freest and best-educated, and it enjoys a higher life expectancy than Germany or the Netherlands. But most remarkable is that Israelis appear to *love life* and hate death more than any other nation."

A poll conducted by The Washington Institute in June 2015,

showed that just over half – 52 percent – of the Palestinians living in East Jerusalem, would prefer Israeli citizenship if a Palestinian state was to be established. The most commonly cited reasons were improved employment prospects, modern medical services and guaranteed access to comprehensive health insurance – benefits which many already receive as Israeli citizens. In 2009, after completing army service in Israel and having worked for a number of charitable organizations, I established an initiative, NU Campaign, which provides support to Israeli NGOs (Non-Governmental Organizations) using uniquely-designed clothing. As a result of this endeavor, I have had the privilege to meet and encounter first-hand the work of many Israelis and Israeli non-government organizations that operate in the fields of life-saving and humanitarian-relief work, both locally and abroad. I have been personally associated with many initiatives, social causes, and national events, and I have witnessed the humanitarian efforts, care and concern extended by thousands of people. My connection to these ventures, their founders, staff and the throngs of volunteers that assist them have inspired me with their high level of concern, self-sacrifice and desire to better the lives of others. That is an integral part of what makes Israel tick. Stories of philanthropic efforts are certainly not unique to Israel. Most nations subscribe to the belief that good deeds and human concern for others are held in high esteem and appreciated. However, I want to allow readers to appreciate life in Israel and its many benevolent human undertakings to reveal a counterpoint to the current wave of misinfo-ration about Israel and its people.

Israeli society is an amalgam of people from every corner of the earth. It is a true melting-pot with a fusion of geographical origins, ethnicities, cultures and religions. Israelis are known for their "chutzpah," and love to get involved in the lives of others. In Israel, it is not uncommon for a total stranger to approach you on the street and instruct you on how to properly dress your baby or show you the correct way to hold him or her. Your neighbors may knock on your door any time of day or night and ask to borrow a cup of sugar, a few carrots or other items of immediate necessity. They may inquire how much you paid for your house before even knowing your name. People will often jump the queue; drive like maniacs; try to negotiate everything; give poor customer service and do many other bewildering things. But when push comes to shove, Israelis overall are most likely to be the *first* people to respond to a call for help any time of the day or night. When the tough exterior displayed by many Israelis is stripped away it reveals a compassionate heart that is forever giving and caring.

Acknowledgments

I would like to thank all those mentioned in this book for the opportunity to share their stories, and to all the other dedicated individuals who work tirelessly around the clock to make this world a better place. I also want to thank my editor, Cina Coren, who was instrumental in putting this book together, as well as Urim Publications' publisher, Tzvi Mauer and copy-editor Pearl Friedman. I am not a writer by profession and it was only through sheer determination to tell this story that I was able to move forward with this endeavor. Lastly, I want to thank my wife Tova, my children, my parents, parents-in-law and family for their unwavering support in everything I do.

↗ Israeli doctors treat young Syrian girl at
Hadassah Hospital, 2018.
(*Hadassah Medical Organization – HMO*)

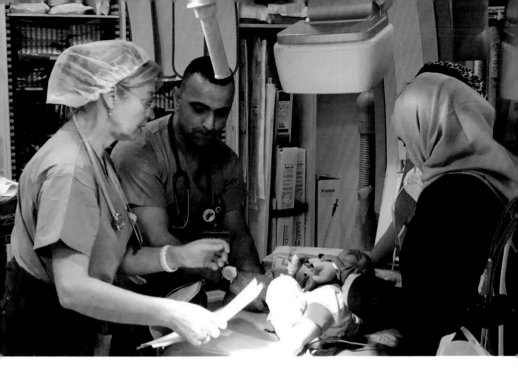

1 "Love Thy Neighbor"
Operation Good Neighbor in Syria

Do not stand idly by while your neighbor's blood is shed.
Leviticus 19:16

Over two thousand years ago a man approached a prominent Jewish leader, Hillel, not far from where I live in Jerusalem and asked that he be taught the entire Torah or Bible while standing on one foot. Hillel answered the man, "What is hateful to you, do not do to your neighbor. That is the whole Torah; the rest is commentary." Many years later, another great Jewish personality Rabbi Akiva echoed these words when he said, "Love your neighbor as yourself, this is a great principle!" Since then, this Biblical statement, with its source in the book of Leviticus (19:18), has become a universal Golden Rule, interpreted thousands of times and taught to Jewish children throughout the generations (and adopted by many other religions as well.) It has also, together with many other Jewish teachings and laws, inspired, influenced and governed the way in which the Jewish people and modern-Israeli-society relates to itself, its communities, neighbors and the countries that surround it.

One related law instructs, "Do not stand idly by while your neighbor's blood is shed (Leviticus 19:16)." So in 2012, when a deadly civil war broke out just over the northern border in Syria, a country whose government still consider Israel its greatest enemy, this directive served as a guiding light to the way in which the government of Israel, The Israeli army (IDF), and thousands of Israeli citizens chose to respond.

In June 2018, a 14-month-old Syrian girl in need of life-saving heart surgery and her young Syrian guardian, arrived at the Israeli-Syrian border for treatment in Israel. The procedure was facilitated by Operation Good Neighbour, a humanitarian aid campaign launched by the Israeli army (IDF) in 2016 with the goal of supporting Syrian civilians, throughout the civil war. The baby was among twenty children referred to a pediatric heart clinic at the Baruch Padeh Medical Center of Poriya Hospital in Tiberias. The northern Israeli hospital partnered with experts in Jerusalem's Hadassah Hospital to treat the children. Dr. Julius Golender, a senior pediatric cardiologist at Hadassah's Ein Kerem campus, travelled to Tiberias and examined the patients. "We can help your daughter," Dr. Golender told the woman as she lovingly held the 14-month old baby born with a ventricular septal defect (VSD), a hole in the wall separating the two lower chambers of the heart. In normal development, the wall between the chambers closes before the baby is born, so that at birth, oxygen-rich blood is kept from mixing with the oxygen-poor blood.

Dr. Golender decided to refer the girl for immediate surgery to Hadassah Ein-Kerem hospital, in Jerusalem. Upon arrival, the Syrian woman met with Sandra Kudsieh, an Arabic-speaking social worker at Hadassah Hospital and told her the whole story of how she secretly took the baby to Tiberias to be examined and then, at night, she rode with the IDF to Jerusalem. She confided to Kudsieh that she was not the mother of the child. "She put me in a difficult position," said Kudsieh. "I had to tell the medical staff that this was an aunt, not a close enough relative to sign the surgery consent papers. But without the surgery, the baby would die." The baby was born to a Syrian couple who split up soon afterwards, partly because of the stress of dealing with such a sick baby. The mother abandoned the baby. The father moved in with his brother and family. His brother's wife treated the baby as her own, even though she was five months pregnant with her fifth child. She took the baby to the doctor, bottle fed her, spent long nights keeping her alive. She had a plan. "Everyone here knows that the Israelis do the complicated surgeries we don't have in Syria. I wanted to save this poor baby who saw me as her mom," she said.

Hadassah pediatric cardio-thoracic surgeon Eldad Erez was ready to perform the operation, but it simply couldn't be done without the parent's permission. As a result, the IDF had the child's father tracked down in Syria and brought to Israel for half an hour. Hadassah doctors spoke to him by Skype to explain the procedure with its risks and benefits. The father signed his consent and the surgery went forward. The next day, the young baby was sitting up and smiling. "I can already see a huge difference," said her aunt.

In 2011, at the outbreak of the war, Israel set up a field hospital adjacent to the Syrian border, to treat those wounded in the conflict. Although Syria has fought several wars against Israel and is considered an openly hostile enemy nation, Israeli army medics have treated thousands of wounded Syrian civilians and rebels, and Israeli hospitals have taken in thousands of Syrian refugee patients. During Operation Good Neighbor, over 1,000 Syrian children were treated in Israel, including 685 in 2017 alone and about a dozen babies were born in Israel to Syrian women. The Israeli Defense Force (IDF) also worked with international organizations and donors to transfer aid to more than 200,000 Syrians living in villages close to the Israeli border. In 2018 alone, some 700 tons of food and flour; 542,880 liters of gas; 174 tons of clothes; 13 generators; 400 items of medical equipment, including incubators and surgery room equipment; and 113 pallets holding 2,214 boxes of medicines were donated to Syrian civilians with the assistance of the IDF. In addition, 6,351 packages of diapers were sent across the border as well as 600 meters of piping to re-establish ruined water infrastructure, providing running water to 5,000 people in the villages. Mobile caravans were also delivered to Syrians across the border to serve as clinics and classrooms. While most of this humanitarian aid was donated by NGOs from around the world, much of it was directly provided by the Israeli government and Israeli citizens.

Additionally, some 200 Israeli volunteers working for an Israeli nonprofit IL4Syrians have been secretly operating in Syria since the beginning of the civil war. They have delivered food, medical supplies, sanitation kits, baby powder, survival kits and even 3,000 protective suits for doctors treating victims of chemical attacks. Volunteers – made up of Israeli Jews, Christians and Muslims – undertake these missions at great risk to their own lives, confronting possible death or being kidnapped by warring factions. In fact, they are required to sign a form stipulating that should they be captured the government will not negotiate for their release.

In December 2016, as Syrian government forces concluded an operation to recapture East Aleppo – an area in rebel hands since 2012 – Syrian President Bashar al-Assad, accused "Israel alone" of being Syria's enemy. In his interview with the Syrian newspaper Al-Watan, Assad neglected to mention that at least 384 Syrian civilians, including 45 children, had been killed by government fire during the siege, along with reports of significant war crimes committed by his troops. That same week an Israeli grass-roots campaign entitled, "Just Beyond the Border," raised over 600,000 shekels for Syrian children in Aleppo. The initiative was supported by thousands of Israelis from all walks of life. Israeli Flying Aid, an Israeli humanitarian-aid organization, was designated to deliver the much needed food and supplies that were donated during the campaign. The project was coordinated by Israelis from across the country including religious and secular Jews, Muslims and Christians, who together organized a mass prayer for the victims of the Syrian conflict during the Jewish fast day of Yom Kippur. "As an Israeli child, I grew up asking where were the people of the world when we needed them most," said organizer Yoav Bakshi Yeivin. "As a Jew, I always knew that I was expected to be there, to help and lend a hand. There is no nation that knows better than us how lethal apathy can be."

In April 2016, the medical staff at Haifa's Rambam Hospital in the north of Israel, treated a five-year-old Syrian girl with severe injuries received as a result of being caught in a crossfire between two warring Syrian militias. Rambam hospital has, over the past few years, been one of the major Israeli hospitals treating Syrians wounded in the war, as part of Operation Good Neighbor. What gave this particular child's story a unique twist is what happened after she was treated for her wounds. Doctors at the hospital discovered that the child also suffered from cancer and needed an urgent bone marrow transplant to save her life. The doctors refused to issue the child's release from their care until she had been treated. To this end, Israel's security services helped to locate one of the girl's relatives in Syria who proved to be a match for a bone marrow transplant. They brought the family member to Israel and thus saved the girl's life.

In June 2018 I participated in a meeting at Jerusalem's Hadassah Hospital, between a Syrian mother who had brought her baby to Israel for life-saving treatment and a visiting delegation from America. The Syrian was the mother of eight children and had left her other seven children in uncertain circumstances while bringing her very sick baby to Israel for medical care. During our meeting facilitated by a translator three things became clear: Firstly, she had risked her life to be in Israel as they had travelled through very dangerous territory in Syria in order to cross the Israel-Syrian border; Secondly, the hospital staff had not only saved her child's life but had taken care of their every need including the purchase of toiletries, food and additional clothing and she was extremely grateful for this; and lastly, she would probably never tell anyone back in Syria that she had ever come to Israel as she would be risking her life if Syrian authorities ever found out.

Although most Syrians who have received help from Israelis are afraid to speak about their experiences due to fear of being found out by the Syrian regime or other rebel groups, amongst other reasons, one Syrian refugee was uninhibited to go public: After Syrian government forces began shelling Aboud Dandachi's neighborhood in September 2013, the 39-year old Sunni Muslim high-tech professional left his birthplace, Homs, for Lebanon and made his way to Istanbul, Turkey. He never imagined the civil war in Syria would last as long as it has. Five years into the war and based on his own personal experiences, Dandachi, has reached one clear conclusion – that Israel is not at all the "Great Satan" he was brought up believing. Quite the opposite, in fact. In December 2015, after witnessing first-hand Israeli assistance toward Syrians fleeing the war, he created a website and launched an online campaign, "in appreciation of the assistance given to Syrian refugees by Israeli and Jewish organizations and individuals." Dandachi's website tells the tales of Jews and Israelis who have helped and who continue to help the Syrian people.

"There are so many stories that I want to put up," he told me. Speaking with him on Skype from my home in Jerusalem, it is difficult to ignore the contrast between my life and the difficult journey and experiences he has faced since the outbreak of the civil war in his home country. A friendly conversation between a Syrian and Israeli should not be taken for granted, as a decade ago, this would have been unheard of.

"There are new stories of Israelis helping Syrians every day. As

Aboud Dandachi, Syrian Refugee. (*Jodi Hilton*)

far as I'm concerned, because we as Syrians cannot give back to Jews what they give to us, we should at least thank them." When I asked him what his family and friends think about what he is doing, he answers, "Things are very tense." Dandachi described the extent to which his opinion of Israel and Israelis has changed. He told me how during the Second Lebanon War in 2006, he celebrated Hezbollah's attacks, hoping that each rocket they fired toward Israel would inflict as much damage as possible. He told me "As a Syrian, I am morally obligated to ensure that the goodwill that Israelis and Jews have displayed towards my people will not be overlooked nor forgotten. The day will come when the conflict in Syria will come to an end, as all things come to an end. On that day, it is imperative that Syrians reciprocate the enormous goodwill shown towards us by Israelis and the Jewish people. Whatever supposed reasons we may have had to be adversaries is dwarfed by the compassion shown to us during our darkest days, a time when we have nothing to give back except our gratitude . . . I grew up hearing statements such as 'These people are your enemies. The Jews are evil.' And then I saw that the Jews and Israelis are the most humane and generous people of this era."

Israelis also responded to the needs of Syrian civilians in June 2018, when the Israel Defense Forces (IDF) delivered humanitarian aid to Syrian refugees at four different locations on its southern border with Israel, in a special overnight operation. Tens of thousands of Syrians fled a massive bombardment in the country's south as the government of President Bashar Al-Assad began a ground offensive to recapture rebel-held areas. The Israeli operation took place over several hours in which 300 tents, 13 tons of food, 15 tons of baby food, three pallets of medical equipment and medicine, along with thirty tons of clothing were transferred to several thousands of Syrian civilians fleeing the hostilities. The supplies had been donated by Israeli communities along the northern border.

"The IDF has provided life-saving humanitarian aid to Syrian civilians through Operation Good Neighbor for several years, as a good-will gesture, while maintaining a policy of non-intervention in the Syrian conflict," the IDF said. "The initiative's activities have been strengthened in light of the difficult situation facing civilians living in the Syrian Golan Heights."

One month later, Israeli forces rescued hundreds of White Helmet volunteers and their family members, trapped and threatened by advancing Syrian regime forces, fleeing to Jordan. Founded in 2013, the Syria Civil Defense, or White Helmets, is a network of first responders who rescue the wounded in the aftermath of air strikes, shelling or explosions in rebel-held territory. The Israeli rescue was praised by Western countries and the operation was described as "out of the ordinary" and "exceptional."

Unfortunately and ironically, Operation Good Neighbor came to a conclusion in December 2018, as Syrian governmental forces once again regained control over the border crossing between Israel and Syria preventing any further cooperation between Israel and the Syrian people.

IsraAid volunteers assisting Syrian refugees as they disembark at the Greek island of Lesbos.
(Main photo: Martin Devesik. Inset: Lior Sperandeo)

2 Guardian "Angels"
A Global Response

To Save a Life is to save an entire world.　　　*Talmud*

In May 2012 Israeli mountain climber and photographer Nadav Ben Yehuda was only 300 meters from the summit of Mount Everest and on his way to becoming the youngest Israeli to climb the world's highest mountain, when he spotted someone lying inside a crack in the ice, clearly in trouble. He recognized Aydin Irmak, a Turkish climber he had first met down at base camp lying unconscious in the ice. He had no oxygen system, gloves or shelter. At the time, more than 200 climbers were also making the ascent to Everest, trying to reach the top before the weather deteriorated. Set on reaching the summit, or just too exhausted by the altitude, they passed right by Aydin without offering to help. With time running out and in the darkness,

Nadav Ben Yehuda, Israeli mountain climber. *(Nadav Ben Yehuda)*

Nadav abandoned the goal he had been training himself for over the past two years and stopped his ascent. He connected Irmak to his harness and held him, as together they descended for eight hours, in complete darkness and in minus 60 degrees centigrade temperature (minus 76 degrees Fahrenheit), until Nadav's fourth rest-camp at 8,050 meters. During those hours, Nadav's oxygen system broke, and his right hand became paralyzed from severe frostbites. From that point it took 23 more hours to reach camp number two (6,450 meters), the highest point a helicopter could land in the harsh conditions. From there, they were both evacuated to Base Camp, and then back to Kathmandu for medical treatment. As a result of the rescue, Nadav lost 19kg of his body weight, and was at great risk of amputation of his right-hand fingers, and parts of his toes from both feet. When interviewed several days later by an Israeli paper, Ben Yehuda said "It was very hard to carry him because he was very heavy. At times he would regain consciousness, and then faint again. When he woke up he would scream in pain, which made it even more difficult. If I had continued climbing, he would have died for certain. Other climbers just passed him by but I had no second thoughts. I knew that I had to save him."

"I would have died on the mountain. It was a miracle . . ." Irmak said. "I remember falling down. I woke up with Nadav standing over me and shouting my name. Nadav did a great thing. He built a bridge between Turkey and Israel, and our leaders can learn a lot from him. . . . I may have missed the summit, but I gained a new brother." For publicity-shy Nadav, who went on to receive a Presidential Medal of Honor from the late president Shimon Peres, the decision to save the life of 46-year-old Aydin Irmak was automatic. In a telephone interview with the Associated Press from Nepal, Ben Yehuda attributed his decision in part to his military training in Israel. "You never leave a man in the field," he said. "A person's life, any person's life, is more valuable than anything else."

Before being presented the Medal of Honor, Ben Yehuda tried to dodge the ceremony saying "I heard about the people who received this medal, and I don't think I am in the same caliber. Some of these people did amazing things."

As Nadav demonstrated, the collective solicitude and compassion inherent within the Israeli psyche is not only limited to those living within and near Israel's borders but is also given to people and nations worldwide, including countries that have diplomatic relations with Israel and those that do not. Israel's efforts to reach out and build bridges with other countries is part of its ongoing determination to provide humanitarian assistance to anyone in need, no matter who they are or where they are from.

In August 1953, several months after Israel celebrated its fifth anniversary, neighboring Greece was devastated by one of the most powerful earthquakes that Europe had ever seen. Israel was still a struggling nation then, plagued by an economic recession and continued military threats from its enemies. The country was also occupied with absorbing waves of immigrants who had arrived from Arab lands and post-Holocaust Europe. Israel's international position was also precarious. Despite its recognition as a bona fide independent nation by many countries, there were still a number of European countries that had not yet recognized Israel because of the Arab boycott, including Germany, Austria, Ireland, Portugal, Spain, and Greece. The newly formed Israeli Navy was in the process of building up its force, with only a small number of old frigate-class warships which had been renovated and put into service together with a mixed assemblage of young sailors who lacked experience and proper naval training. On August 12, 1953, the Israeli flotilla was on its way back to Israeli shores after four weeks of intense training in the Aegean Sea when suddenly it heard S.O.S alerts being sent off the Greek shores. A series of deadly earthquakes, measuring 7.3 on the Richter scale, had struck the area of the Greek islands Kefalonia, Zante and Ithaca. The commander of the Israeli flotilla reported back to naval headquarters in Haifa and requested permission to turn back and offer aid. The Israeli response was immediate: "Enter and provide assistance." The Israeli fleet sailed right past the American and British fleets which, because of the huge size of their warships, could not access the areas that had been hit. In his blog "Seven Seas – notes from the Great Blue," Yiftach Kozik who was a naval officer aboard the ship at the time, vividly described the sights encountered by the Israeli naval personnel upon their arrival at the devastated islands: "Huge clods of earth were falling into the water at tremendous speeds, the summit of Mount Ainos on the island of Kefalonia looked as though it was split in two . . . and fierce fires had broken out in the olive oil storerooms and were burning all that remained. . . . In most of the island's village not a building remained standing, and thousands were wounded in critical condition, among them pregnant women, old and young, people with amputated and crushed limbs. . . . The Israeli teams performed emergency surgeries: a broken pelvis, skull fractures, premature births, complex fractures, hemorrhages, panic attacks, despair, and havoc everywhere. . . ." The United Nations Convention on the Law of the Sea at that time stipulated that the first rescue force to arrive on an emergency scene assumes responsibility for the rescue operation. Since the Israeli navy was the first to land on the shores of Kefalonia, it immediately took charge while also directing the rescue operations of the American and British fleets. It took three days and nights for the 450 Israeli sailors working alongside the Americans and the British to provide relief to the residents of the Greek islands, transporting hundreds of seriously wounded casualties to the mainland, and providing medical assistance to thousands of local residents. The Greek government had not yet recognized the state of Israel, and official recognition would only happen 37 years later, but the Greek people expressed their gratitude in other ways. The king of Greece paid a personal visit to the navy soldiers to convey a message of thanks to David Ben Gurion, Israel's Prime Minister, and to award badges of merit to the commanders of the operation, Shlomo Harel and Yizhak Dviri. In an act of appreciation for the Israeli navy, the Greek media referred to the group as "the fleet of love and hope," and "the Israeli sailors of salvation."

This act of heroism of the Navy soldiers served as the first Israeli humanitarian aid operation in a disaster zone and it laid the foundation for a long tradition of global Israel aid missions which have become part and parcel of the Jewish State today. Since then, the Israeli government has become deeply committed to humanitarian relief efforts and international development programs throughout the world and Israel is *always* amongst the first countries to offer international aid to countries struck by natural and unnatural disasters including those countries that have diplomatic relations with Israel and those that do not. The State of Israel has to date sent over 140 official aid missions to over 50 countries. These delegations include medical experts, search and rescue teams and trauma councilors. They are sent by the Israeli government, the Israeli Defense Force and many other Israeli volunteer-based organizations that have become first responders to disaster areas worldwide, in their desperate time of need.

Today Israel enjoys very close relations with Greece but there are still many countries, including Islamic-nations, which do not recognize or have official relations with Israel and in some cases much of the Western world. When disasters strike these areas, their leaders often prevent lifesaving aid from reaching their own people, causing even greater consequences. However, there are some Israelis and Israeli organizations who will stop at nothing to go beyond their call of duty, to provide assistance to these populations when disaster strikes.

Cyclone Nargis hit Myanmar (formerly Burma) in 2008, killing over twenty thousand men, women and children and affecting close to 1.5 million people. Gal Lusky, founder of Israeli Flying Aid, an Israeli life-saving aid organization whose mission is to bring vital supplies and aid to people in far flung disaster areas worldwide, watched closely on television as the events unfolded. Initial reports indicated that the military regime of Myanmar refused any international aid to its people. Unlike other aid organizations, the IFA focuses on people in remote locations around the globe, who are either intentionally or unintentionally overlooked by most government or international aid organizations. I met Gal in a crowded café in Tel-Aviv in 2010. In the comfort of the restaurant, it is hard to imagine the many life endangering humanitarian missions that she and her team of volunteers have undertaken to help the most desperate people in the world. In Myanmar, Gal and her team followed the IFA mandate, that in spite of the ban, they would arrange a secret mission to bring vital supplies to the people of Myanmar. Gal's team purchased aid packages upon ar-

Israeli Flying Aid volunteer cheers up kids in Disaster zone *(Israeli Flying Aid)*

riving in Myanmar and convinced a local truck driver, who risked his own imprisonment, to escort them to the areas affected by the disaster. Before departing, they piled bags of rice in the back of the vehicle, to provide them cover, should they be stopped by government forces. The journey was an anxious one. At one point, they passed through a military check-point with everyone in the truck ducking down in the back. After passing much devastation on the roads, with dead live-stock, trees and debris scattered all over the roads, they arrived at a village where hundreds of starving people instantly surrounded their truck. They are clearly the first aid group to have arrived. To instill a semblance of control among the desperate crowd, the Israeli team told the masses to sit down and they then proceeded to distribute the much-needed food. There wasn't enough to go around and some people were left hungry. Gal explained that she couldn't understand why the government was not helping its own people, "It's like Genocide," she said.

Gal explained her motivations for starting Israeli Flying Aid. "The IFA does not discriminate between disaster victims based on their race, religion, the hostility of their governments toward Israel, and not even in the face of anti-Semitism. When I leave my son to fly off to a new dangerous destination, I don't think of it as a choice. When I hug him goodbye, I know that I am fulfilling a responsibility that I did not choose. Rather, it chose me. As a woman who loves her country, a Jew who knows about the tragedies of the Holocaust, and a sister with a brother wounded in war, I see my team's mission to bring aid wherever it may be needed, not necessarily wherever its allowed, as doing our small part to bring about Tikkun Olam, the Jewish ideal of fixing (or, in this case, healing) the world. Though the mission seems too great for me at times, as a mother, I feel it is my responsibility to leave the world a more tolerant place than when I found it. . . . We go where no one else will go because of politics, danger, or governmental blocks. We have flown to Indonesia, the country with the largest number of Muslims in the world, provided aid behind the lines of governmental blockades in Myanmar and fed Georgians during Russia's occupation. We fly around the world with the Star of David on our chests (when it is at all possible,) and often operate in disguise amongst local populations, seeking to help wherever we can. . . . putting our lives at risk to assist absolute strangers, some of whom might even consider themselves our enemies. Yet, for Israelis, this comes naturally. . . . Building the State of Israel was a gamble taken by the Jewish people to change the course of their own history. And it worked. We therefore feel a responsibility to provide aid to others in similar situations, [people] facing tragedy and abandonment by the world and to do everything in our power to help them rebuild their lives. . . . As a nation, we have stood both at the height of leadership and at the bottom rungs of the societal ladder. The role we can take globally is one of teaching, showing the world that compassion is key. Because ultimately, the distance between the highest and the lowest points on the societal ladder is as small as a single natural or man-made disaster. . . . When we are asked why we help populations around the world rather than just focusing our attention on Israel, we explain that Jewish law demands respect for human life above all else. When we seek global betterment, we should pay no attention to politics. Even if someone is a Kashmiri rebel, there is no reason to allow their children to freeze to death. In Israel, we do not choose between human lives based on citizenship and allegiance. We work under the presumption that every life is worth saving. Period. Conflict and politics simply should not come into play. After all, we are trying to fix one shared world."

In Myanmar alone, Israeli Flying Aid provided 80,000 people with food. Yet, 360,000 people died of starvation after the 2007 cyclone. The organization has also been instrumental in supplying aid and medical treatment to refugees and citizens in Syria throughout the civil war. The IFA slogan is, "No one asks permission to be killed, so we don't ask permission to save lives." Gal's team is made up of over 1200 volunteers including medical experts, search and rescue personal and psycho-trauma specialists. They drop their work at any moment to fly across the world following global disasters. ". . . We are loyal first to our own sense of consciousness and values and then to the victim's needs. Nothing in between."

In the past decade the world has witnessed some of the deadliest natural disasters of the century, devastating populations indiscriminately across the globe. Throughout all these tragic events, from hurricanes to earthquakes, landslides to tsunamis, the one thing that has been consistent– besides the obvious destruction – is that the State of Israel and its citizens are always amongst the first nations to touch down and assist on the ground, no matter where these tragedies take place.

When 22-year-old Emmanuel Bito was pulled barely-alive from the rubble of a three-story building ten days after a devastating earthquake struck the island of Haiti in 2010, the first faces he saw were those of the Israeli rescue workers who had flown across the world to help. A search conducted by the Israeli army's Home Front Command, headed by Lt. Col. Rami Peletz was directed to Emmanuel's location by local residents. American and French doctors had been unable to rescue Bito and they called upon the Israeli delegation's search and rescue teams who succeeded in rescuing him from a three-meter long tunnel, within half an hour. When asked by a journalist how he felt following the event, Lt. Col Peletz quoted a traditional Jewish Talmudic passage, "When you save a life, it's is as if you saved the entire world."

In Haiti, over 100,000 people were killed as a result of the disaster and over one million people lost their homes. Israel was the first country to provide aid to the disaster struck region. A CNN reporter toured the Israeli field hospital which was set up in coordination with the Haitian Ministry of Defense. He commented that Israel had begun treating hundreds of patients before any other country had even arrived on the scene. The Israeli rescue crew had set up the largest technologically sophisticated medical facility in Haiti, including a medical lab, pharmacy and an x-ray center. With over 250 doctors and search and rescue personal they treated more than 1,110 patients, conducted 319 successful

IDF search and rescue soldiers pulling Emmanuel Bito from rubble in Haiti, 2010
(*Israel Defense Forces*)

surgeries and delivered 16 babies including three by Caesarian sections.

In November 2016, WHO, the World Health Organization, following several months of vetting, granted the IDF field hospital level 3 status, the highest possible ranking. It was the only field hospital ever to receive this status. One of the features that sets the Israeli field hospital apart is a novel system that provides each patient with his/her own digital medical file. Patients who arrive at the field hospital are greeted by a medical assistant who takes a picture and gives each one a unique barcode which is scanned at every station the patient goes through allowing the doctor to access all medical information and treatments the patient receives. This system ensures the Israeli team that no station in the hospital is overwhelmed with patients and that quality treatment remains a top priority.

In one incident at the Israeli field hospital in Haiti, a resident of Port-au-Prince, the Haitian Capitol, gave birth to a son. As a token of appreciation and gratitude, she named him "Israel" in honor of the country that helped her. Soon after that, Mike, a four-year-old Haitian boy, was brought to the IDF field hospital by his father because of vomiting and weakness. Mike, his two siblings and his parents, had been living on the street since the earthquake because their house was destroyed. Israeli doctors ran blood tests and diagnosed him with acute myelogenous leukemia. Mike needed chemotherapy and a bone marrow transplant, a long and complex process. His condition was urgent and the IDF medical team arranged for him to be sent to America for treatment.

And in another search and rescue mission in Haiti, an eight-story university building in Port-au-Prince collapsed and trapped eight students underneath the rubble. The students' cries could be heard from outside and the Haitian military did everything they could to locate the young Haitians. Soon after the rescue operation began, members of ZAKA, a leading Israeli rescue and recovery NGO, were dispatched to the scene and took control. The six-man Israeli delegation had arrived in Haiti aboard a Mexican air force Hercules, immediately after completing their work in the recovery and identification efforts following a helicopter crash in Mexico City, which had occurred days before the earthquake in Haiti. They quickly made their way to the university building and after 38 hours of working around the clock with the Mexican military delegation and other Jewish volunteers from Mexico, they succeeded in rescuing the students alive from the rubble. The collapse took place on a Saturday, the Jewish Sabbath, and amid the wreckage and chaos, the ZAKA delegation took time out to recite Shabbat prayers. This led to the strange sight of Jewish Orthodox men wrapped in prayer shawls standing amongst the destroyed structures. At that point large crowds of Haitians gathered at the site and stared in shock at the men as they prayed facing Jerusalem. They told the Israelis that they looked like angels who had come to save their fellow countrymen. When the prayers ended, the local people crowded around the ZAKA delegation and kissed their prayer shawls.

Another group of Israelis to arrive immediately in Haiti in the aftermath of the earthquake were members of the Herzog Israel Center for the Treatment of Psychotrauma (ICTP), an NGO that extends psychotrauma assistance in the immediate and long-term aftermath of traumatic events. In addition to its work in Israel, the ICTP, founded in 1989 by Dr. Danny Brom, collaborates with specialists around the world to develop and share its unique expertise. Shortly after returning from assisting in Haiti following the earthquake in 2010, Dr. Brom told me that, "It doesn't take much to realize why Israelis, unfortunately, are experts in trauma and resilience. A history of wars and our ongoing struggle against terrorism has necessitated and facilitated much needed knowledge and experience in this area." The posters in the ICTP headquarters are testimony to the hardships and struggles that many Israeli's have endured since Israel's establishment.

Between the years 1977–1984, during a wave of Ethiopian immigration to Israel, which culminated in the Israeli airlift rescue mission Operation Moses, many immigrants, including entire families with little children undertook long and dangerous treks which often lasted for months, from their homes in Ethiopian villages to temporary camps in Sudan where they were airlifted by Israeli planes. As a result of the difficult journey and bad conditions, facing disease, hunger and attacks by bandits, approximately 4,000 Beta Israel Ethiopian Jews died on the way. Those that survived the journey arrived in Israel and had to cope with the drastic transition, moving from rural life in Africa to a modern technology-driven country and society.

In Haiti, the ICTP helped establish a school-based intervention program, which was adopted by local Haitian partners. The program trained teachers to strengthen the resilience of children and prepared local professionals to identify and treat youth suffering from psycho-trauma, a devastating and demoralizing result of these disasters.

Although Israel is a tiny country, no bigger than the state of New Jersey or Lake Michigan, Israeli aid organizations and official government missions have provided humanitarian assistance on many occasions to their bigger friends, including the United States, helping them through some of the most traumatic experiences in recent years. When Hurricane Katrina flooded and devastated New Orleans in 2005, Israel took an active role in supporting the victims. Immediately following the disaster, the Israel Foreign Ministry put out an urgent call for all businesses and organizations to donate essential goods to the hurricane victims. Some Israeli organizations, such as Magen David Adom set up special funds with the sole purpose of sending monetary contributions to the victims. The Hebrew University in Jerusalem and Tel-Aviv University offered scholarships and shortened the acceptance process for students from Tulane University in New Orleans, Louisiana, which was forced to shut down and cancel its fall semester. With the death toll reaching in the thousands and with 80% of New-Orleans under water, IsraAID, (The Israel

Forum for International Humanitarian Aid) – Israel's leading humanitarian non-profit that specializes in disaster response and international development – sent a private delegation of divers to New Orleans to search for bodies in flooded homes.

IsraAID was founded in 2001 to aggregate Israeli expertise and knowledge and share it with the world. To date they have responded to crises in 47 countries, delivering over 1,000 tons of relief and medical supplies to over 1.5 million people. In New Orleans, the 25 members of IsraAID were armed with high-power flashlights to search for bodies in the dark, contaminated waters. Several days into the ordeal, the Israelis were working with a local fire department team when they learned that one of the firefighters, a man named Ervin, had lived in a house on the street they were clearing. As it turned out, the firefighters had checked Ervin's house the previous day but he didn't have the heart to go in and survey the damage. "So I took him hand-in-hand to his house," said Sarit Vino Elad, an Israeli singer-actress who also works in psychodrama. "It was another ruined, muddy, ugly house but for him it was home. He was looking at his house, at his wife's china collection, at his dining room. His cat was dead on the couch in the living room." The place was badly damaged but Ervin was pleased to find that his bed, which his wife had made before evacuating, was still made and her silk pajamas were lying neatly on the comforter. In the attic, where the heat was especially intense, the only thing that had escaped destruction was a case of family photographs Ervin had stowed away before Katrina hit. "He opened the box of pictures and on the top of the box was a picture of him and his wife on their wedding day and he burst into tears," she recalled.

Working alongside American search and rescue teams, another Israeli aid worker recounted that the soldiers were shocked to see them. They asked us, "How come you came from so far? You have your own troubles. You're such a small country." The answer was, "We're a small country but with big friends. For us it was so obvious. America has been such a good friend of ours for so long. How can we not offer our help when it is needed?"

Hurricane Katrina was not the only time that Israel arrived on US soil to help in the aftermath of a local disaster. After a terror attack at the finish line of the Boston Marathon on April 15, 2013, three people were killed and at least 264 injured. Law enforcement officials from Israel flew to Boston to help with the investigation and a number of Israelis and Israeli organizations helped Bostoners cope with the aftermath of the tragedy. The Israel Trauma Coalition (ITC) led a team of experts to Massachusetts and held workshops for emergency workers, medical professionals, schools and religious leaders.

"In their greatest hour of despair, people do have their own strengths and you need to strengthen [boost] them," said ITC director Talia Levanon. "We bring with us the understanding that we've been through this and continue to hold our values both professionally and as individuals. We also remind people: 'You will survive this.' Ours is a message of resiliency and hope that needs to be fostered in people," she said.

The experience that Israelis gain in the army is a major factor that influences their life decisions after their military service. In Israel, most Israeli teenagers, both male and female, are conscripted into the army or volunteer in national institutions countrywide after high-school and spend 2–3 years of their lives serving their country in some capacity. The values they learn during this period including leadership, responsibility, comradeship, loyalty, truth, honesty, friendship stay with them for life and express themselves in different ways when they re-enter society at the end of their service.

Rabbi Micha Odenheimer, founder of Tevel b'Tzedek, with Pashupatinath temple Baba, Kathmandu. *(Tevel b'Tzedek)*

Micha Odenheimer, a rabbi and a prolific journalist, traveled to Nepal in 2005, where he encountered large numbers of Israeli tourists who were visiting the impoverished nation. "These were not just backpackers trekking around the country looking for fun. They were talented and motivated young adults who, upon witnessing the devastating poverty in the country, were compelled to do something to help. They lamented the fact that there was no framework at the time in which they could do so," said Micha. Every year about 40,000 young Israeli's hang up their boots after finishing the army and head off to exotic, far-flung locations in the Far East, Africa and South America. Micha, with previous experience providing humanitarian aid in developing nations, listened to what returning Israelis had to say and began thinking about a way to funnel the energy and curiosity of these young

Tevel b'Tzedek volunteers in Nepal.
(Shay Wagner Photography)

Israelis to help the world's poorest and most marginalized communities. When he returned to Israel he raised seed money and recruited 15 young Israelis who were up to the challenge. In 2007, they moved to the Swayambu neighborhood in Kathmandu, living in a group house and volunteering with local NGOs. Micha remained with the group, mentoring their work and inspiring them with study sessions on how Jewish and universal philosophy can act as a source of motivation. This first group was the start of the Tevel b'Tzedek movement that has, in the past 9 years, sent over 800 young Israelis and Jews to Nepal to contribute and to learn. These young leaders have returned to their home communities with a different view of the world and their place in it. The organization has grown exponentially and become a recognized and leading INGO (international NGO) in Nepal, the only Israeli organization with that status. To date, it employs a staff of 60 Nepali employees, and runs a variety of groundbreaking projects in agriculture, education, income generation and women's empowerment that impact over 25,000 rural villagers.

On April 25, 2015, when a 7.8 magnitude earthquake devastated the very communities where Tevel had been working for the past several years, the Tevel staff and volunteers were instrumental in distributing crucial emergency supplies and aid to local communities and villages. Tevel's intricate knowledge of Nepal, its INGO status, its highly professional Nepalese staff and relationships with governmental and local communities put the organization in a unique position to help in the long-term recovery.

Purna, a 50-year old Nepalese victim of the earthquake and his family were among the thousands of Nepalese that received aid from Tevel in the days after the disaster. He was working in a nearby stone quarry when the earthquake hit. He ran home and found his family huddled around the ruins of their home, devastated. They spent the night together shivering in the rain and cold in a makeshift tent. Not long after the quake, Purna and his family received tin roofing from Tevel. Despite nationwide shortages, Tevel managed to acquire and distribute the desperately needed building materials within a short time. In a letter penned to Tevel staff, Purna wrote, "Your organization was sent by God for earthquake victims like us. We haven't rebuilt our house yet, but at least we have sturdy temporary shelters. There is a shortage of building materials and of course, money. Even if we had money to buy tin roofing sheets, there aren't any in the market. Thank you."

Tevel also provided critical logistical support to the Israeli embassy and to the Israeli government official aid mission numbering 260 people, one of the largest groups in Nepal to date.

The mission, comprised of doctors and search and rescue personnel, set up a field hospital of 60 beds, treated 1,600 patients, carried out 85 life-saving surgeries, and delivered eight babies. It included members of the Israeli organizations Magen-David Adom, ZAKA, IsrAID and Dream Doctors. After the initial aid, Tevel signed a 3-year agreement with the government of Nepal for an ambitious, 3-year recovery program to help 20,000 villagers in areas destroyed by the earthquake. Together with partners such as the American Jewish Joint Distribution Committee and Magen David Adom, Tevel is not just giving initial first aid, but is ensuring that the villages recover and thrive in the long term.

The Israeli Defense Forces also responded immediately in September 2017, in the aftermath of a lethal 7.1 magnitude earthquake that struck Mexico City. As in almost every other recent natural disaster, Israel extended its support to the Latin American country and sent an IDF delegation to assist victims of the disaster. The IDF aid mission was called *"Shofar's* Call to the Distance," because it took place during the Jewish New Year, when a ram's horn or *shofar* is used in synagogues. It included a team of 70 soldiers and officers in mandatory and reserve duty, from both the Israel Air Force and the Home Front Command. Over 270 people died in the earthquake, more than 1,900 were injured and thousands of those lost their homes. Local Mexicans showed great appreciation for the Israeli team as crowds of people, including other search and rescue teams, lined the streets and spontaneously cheered as uniformed Israeli rescue workers arrived at the disaster zone. The foreign minister of Mexico hailed the Israeli delegation and requested that they extend their stay.

The Israeli government and NGOs have provided aid and first responders to many other recent disasters worldwide, including:

- Hurricane Matthew; October 2016
- Flooding, Uruguay and Paraguay; January 2016
- Flooding, United Kingdom; January 2016
- Flooding, the Carolinas; October 2015
- Flooding, Myanmar; August 2015
- Tornado, Illinois; July 2015
- Cyclone Pam, Vanuatu; March 2015
- Typhoon Haiyan, Philippines; November 2013
- Typhoon Haiyan, Philippines; November 2013
- Typhoon Ruby, Philippines; December 2014
- Flooding, Serbia and Bosnia; May 2014
- Hurricane Sandy, Eastern United States; November 2012
- Hurricane Katrina, New Orleans; 2005
- Typhoon Parma, Philippines; 2009

↗ Sivan Borowich-Yaari, founder of Innovation: Africa. *(Innovation: Africa)*

3 "Light unto Africa"
A Vision of Zionism

Like them [Africans], we had to learn how to increase the yields of our crops, how to irrigate, how to raise poultry, how to live together and how to defend ourselves. . . .
Golda Meir

During a meeting at the Israel Ministry of Foreign Affairs in 1959, fifteen foreign servicemen sat at attention in front of Golda Meir, the Israeli Foreign Minister at the time and later Israel's first woman Prime Minister, often referred to as the "Iron Lady" of politics. Golda professed to them the moral obligation that the Jewish State bore for assisting the countries in Africa.

"Coming to the aid of the newly independent African states is an emotional thing for me. It is a drive toward universal self-determination and justice which lies at the very heart of my Labor

Zionism. Indeed, my African policy is a logical extension of the socialist Zionist principles in which I have always believed." She went on to compare the centuries-long suffering of the Jewish nation with that of the African people, citing the years of discrimination, oppression and slavery endured by both peoples. And then she pointed to the book she was holding, *Altneuland* (Old-New Land), written in 1902 by the founder of the Zionist movement, Dr. Theodor Herzl. In it, Dr. Herzl describes the Jewish state of the future as he imagined it might be and he mentions specifically the African question and helping the developing world. Golda continued by admitting that she had taken on the responsibility to carry out Dr. Theodor Herzl's vision. With more and more African states gaining national independence each year, each one can benefit from Israel's vast amount of expertise, she said. The foreign minister went on to declare that with the full backing of the government, Israel was going to send thousands of Israeli experts of every sort – technologists, scientists, doctors, engineers, teachers, agronomists and irrigation experts in order to share their know-how with the African people.

The incidence of poverty in Africa today stands at more than 218 million people and this figure is increasing faster than the population, creating one of the most pressing human rights issue of our time. Since Israel's establishment, a large part of its foreign aid effort has focused on the African continent and much of the developing world. Since Israel is a country where the majority of land is desert with limited annual rainfall, it has had to rely on creative solutions for a sufficient water supply throughout its existence and as a result it has become a global leader in sanitation and water supply technology, innovations that are needed for similar conditions in Africa and other parts of the developing world. Currently, 2.4 billion people in the world face severe water short-

Young girl fetching water enabled by Innovation: Africa. (Innovation: Africa)

ages. Israel recycles 70% of its waste water and sewage. In addition to its major natural water resources – the Sea of Galilee and the mountain and coastal aquifers – Israel already has several desalination plants in operation, and several more are planned. In total, these plants are projected to provide for two-thirds of the country's water needs in the future.

Native-born Israeli, Sivan Ya'ari, landed her first job in Africa in 1998, as the head of quality control for a multinational clothing company. The experience provided her with first-hand exposure to the poverty that exists in the African continent, motivating her to complete a Master's degree in Energy and Environment from Columbia University and start Innovation: Africa, an organization that has so far impacted the lives of over one million African people, granting them access to clean water and energy.

I met Sivan at an incubator for social entrepreneurs in Jerusalem in 2010, where she explained this drive: "Only when I found myself in Africa did I understand what true poverty really meant," Sivan told me. She described the following account of her life-changing moment: "One day I walked to the nearest infirmary, which was about five miles away from the village. Upon my arrival, I discovered a long line of people waiting to be treated. I asked to see the doctor and was told that there are no doctors here. I approached the nurse and asked her about the long line of people waiting for treatment and vaccinations. 'There are no vaccinations or medicines left – they have been spoiled as we do not have a refrigerator to store them. We have no electricity. It was night by the time I made my way back from the clinic and dark-

Solar Panel Installation at Nyanza Primary School in Uganda.

(Innovation: Africa)

ness covered the entire village." Sivan reflected on her experience, remarking that "I have given birth twice in Israel via C-section. Had I lived in Africa, I would not have survived. Many women die during child birth due to severe understaffing and the lack of electricity for light and medical devices. The nurses are using toxic kerosene lamps to provide light during the delivery. When I grasped the situation in the villages, it was difficult for me to remain indifferent to these challenges, especially because the solution seemed so simple."

The more time Sivan spent in Africa and in the villages the more she realized that the main challenge Africa is facing is the lack of energy. Without energy, people do not have access to good healthcare or good education. Crucially, the lack of energy means that people don't have access to water because there is no energy to pump the water up from beneath the ground. The severity of seeing mothers and children searching for water, for hours every day, even digging by hand and drinking whatever they could find, knowing that it will most likely make them sick, made Sivan realize that energy is truly the key solution to solve many of the challenges she saw. After considering the advanced technological efforts and innovations in her native country, Sivan decided to share Israeli technologies and know-how and in 2008, she founded here own organization Innovation: Africa (iA). IA is a 501-c3 non-profit based in New York, with offices in Israel and Africa. The goal was simple and since then, iA has provided energy for light and to pump water using Israeli solar technology to more than 1 million people in communities throughout Ethiopia, Tanzania, Malawi, Uganda, South Africa, Cameroon, the Democratic Republic of Congo, Senegal and Zambia. To date, they have brought light, pumped clean water and installed drip irrigation in over 200 villages. To ensure that the systems are operating effectively they use a custom-designed remote monitoring system that collects data from the solar systems and sends that information to an online server allowing Sivan's team, the donors and the local engineers to monitor all systems, live.

"By knowing how much energy our projects are producing and consuming, we can preempt problems before they even start," explained Sivan. In 2017, Sivan and her team visited Akuyam Village in Uganda. Located in the Nakapirpirit District in the north-east Karamoja Region, it is home to 4,600 people. At the time, the region was suffering from severe drought and famine. When the iA team arrived, they found a horrific situation. Thirty-seven people died of hunger and dehydration that week alone. The only source of water for the community was a pool of dirty and contaminated water which had dried up, forcing women to walk great distances in search of an alternative source, often with no success. Understanding the severity of the situation Sivan and her team for the first time in iA's history, sent trucks of beans and maize from a region six hours away, just to keep the community alive while they started drilling and the building of the solar water tower. Within days, iA had installed 12 taps supplying clean water throughout the village as well as a drip irrigation system which allowed the community to grow food faster, using less water. Through Innovation: Africa's work to harness the energy from the sun and pump water up from forty meters below the ground, the community in Akuyam is now thriving. People are healthier, children are going to school, and most importantly, access to water allows them to grow more food and sell the surplus in the market enabling the community to become self-sufficient and financially independent. This was just one of hundreds of similar installations undertaken by this Israeli NGO.

Many African states in the 1970s, under diplomatic pressure from the Arab world, severed ties with the Jewish State. However, in recent years, there has been a revival of Israeli-African cooperation and collaboration in areas of Israeli medical, agricultural, security and water management.

Following the outbreak of the Ebola virus in parts of Western Africa, which caused global panic and fear, Israel sent three mobile emergency clinics to Sierre-Leon and Liberia to treat people infected by the virus. The clinics were accompanied by a staff of medical experts who trained local practitioners in the operation of the clinic and its equipment. In addition, the staff also focused on preventing the spread of the disease and raising awareness among populations with high potential for infection.

Another time, MASHAV – the Hebrew acronym for Israel's

Agency for International Development Cooperation donated protective suits and tons of vital supplies to combat the deadly bird-flu virus in Ethiopia and Cameroon.

Malaria is another deadly epidemic facing parts of Africa, causing roughly 655,000 deaths per year, mainly among pregnant woman and children. Back in the 1920s in British Mandate Palestine, the name given to Israel before the establishment of the State of Israel in 1948, Jewish immigrants arriving in the country, predominantly from Eastern Europe, faced a similar malaria epidemic, as a result of swamps and marshes that covered many parts of Israel. Through a systematic approach that included not only draining marshes, spraying larva-infested areas and introducing new treatments, but also improving housing conditions and mounting a vast community education effort, Israel succeeded in eradicating the disease. Now, those same methodologies are being revived and taught to African countries, like Gabon and Zanzibar, spearheaded by The Hebrew University in Jerusalem.

On a recent trip to Ethiopia, eight doctors, three nurses and one physical therapist from the Hadassah Medical Organization in Jerusalem travelled on a weeklong medical mission to the city of Mekelle, in the African country's north. Led by Dr. Josh Schroeder, a spine surgeon at Hadassah and Dr. Allon Moses, the chairman of Hadassah's Department of Clinical Microbiology and Infectious Disease, the Israeli medical team performed five surgeries at the Ayder Comprehensive Specialized Hospital. The hospital serves some eight million people but does not have a spine surgeon.

The Ethiopian patients, aged 18 and under, all suffered from

Ethiopian girl being checked by Israeli doctors before spinal surgery, 2018.
(David Kaplan)

twisted spines as a result of various spinal deformities and travelled from far-flung villages to receive the treatment in Mekelle.
Their conditions were critical and were causing potentially lethal
complications, including pressure on internal organs and lung in-
fections. The Israeli doctors assessed that without surgery the patients might die within the year. The surgeries were complex, with
some taking eight hours. In addition to performing the five surgeries, the Israelis also provided medical training to Ayder staff.
The medical device company Medtronic donated the equipment
necessary for the surgeries. The Hadassah and Ayder hospitals
have a partnership dating back many years, with Israeli medical
students doing rotations in Mekelle, and Ayder physicians receiving training and supplies from Hadassah. One of the nurses of the
mission was Tsheay (Orna) Tadoses-Solomon, herself an immigrant to Israel from Ethiopia in the 1980s with Operation Moses.
This was Tadoses-Solomon's first time returning to Ethiopia, al-

beit under very different circumstances – today she is the deputy
head nurse in the recovery room at Hadassah-University Medical
Center on Jerusalem's Mount Scopus. Before conducting the surgeries the Israeli doctors fixed a mezuzah to the doorpost of the
surgery room, as is traditional in all operating rooms in Israel,
because as one of the doctors said, "It's a branch of Hadassah." In
the end, all five surgeries were successful and within the week the
Ethiopian teenagers were able to stand upright and start walking.

Israel is currently at the forefront of healthcare and agricultural
assistance throughout the developing world – not just in Africa.

In July 2015, as the ISIS terror group callously attacked Yazidi
villages, a small religious-minority sect in Iraq. Khairy al-Shingari, a Yazidi, and his son Wassam, in desperate need of life-saving heart surgery, were brought to Israel by the Israeli non-profit
organization, Save a Child's Heart (SACH). Wisam was blue in
the face, from lack of oxygen as a result of his condition. His father waited anxiously throughout his son's seven-hour surgery,
performed by an Israeli medical team at Wolfson Medical Center.
Al-Shingari had a lot on his mind, throughout the surgery. Not
only was he worried about his son but at the same time, he was
desperately trying to learn information about the fate of his wife
and four other children who had fled on foot from the ISIS mas-
sacres. In a CNN report on the incident, he told the reporter,
"There were hundreds of young men and boys and they slaugh-
tered them in the name of religion. What kind of sick people are
these?" he said in disgust. The procedure on his son took place

Iraqi boy Wisam
with his father after
surgery in Israel, 2015.
(Save A Child's Heart)

within a ten-minute drive from the SACH Children's Home, in
Holon, outside Tel-Aviv.

The doctors at Wolfson contribute a substantial portion of their
time without any additional payment from Save a Child's Heart.
"To see a child who is sick and is now no longer sick, I know of
nothing better," said Dr. Houri, Head of the Pediatric Intensive
care Unit at Wolfson, following the successful surgery. Soon af-

ter the operation al Shingari learned that his family back home had survived the assault by entering a Kurdish stronghold nearby.

Save a Child's Heart (SACH) is an Israeli based international humanitarian organization that brings sick children suffering from heart diseases to Israel for free heart surgery. The kids come from underdeveloped countries that lack sufficient medical staff and facilities and they receive the necessary treatment in Israel. SACH also trains medical teams from partner medical facilities in the developing world and creates centers of medical efficiency in these countries. Each child patient is brought to Israel accompanied by a family member and they are housed, fed, entertained and looked after 24 hours a day by a dedicated team of staff, interns and volunteers. Some of them undergo multiple operations and stay in the country for as long as it takes until their lives are restored and are healthy enough to return to their homes.

The organization was founded in 1995 by Dr. Ami Cohen, an American Israeli serving as the Deputy Chief of Cardiovascular Surgery and Head of Pediatric Cardiac Surgery at Wolfson hospital in Israel. Sadly, Ami died in a tragic accident while climbing Mount Kilimanjaro in August of 2001.

His life's project, Save a Child's Heart, transcends national boundaries and political differences, building bridges of peace and understanding between Israel and the world. Today, under the leadership of Dr. Lior Sasson, Dr. Cohen's successor, it is the largest organization of its kind in the world and it has saved the lives of more than 4,000 children from a wide variety of countries in the developing world including Africa, Eastern Europe, and China. Forty perent of the patients come from Muslim countries like Afghanistan, Jordan, Egypt, Iraq and Palestinian controlled areas, such as the Gaza Strip.

Among many other recent humanitarian activities Israel has undertaken in the developing world, here are just a few more examples:

- There are approximately 22 million people currently living in Africa with HIV and AIDS – two-thirds of the entire world's population of HIV. Israel is playing its part to stop the epidemic. Israeli doctors, through an Israeli organization, Operation Abraham, regularly fly to Africa to help train local medical personnel in male medical circumcision in order to prevent further spread of the disease.

- Israeli non-profit, Eye from Zion, sends volunteer eye doctors from Israel to do free cataract removal operations in Africa and places such as Vietnam, China, Myanmar, the Maldives and even Muslim countries including Azerbaijan. The organization also brings doctors from developing countries to Israel for training in eye procedures.

- In July 2014, Israeli firm, Gigawatt Global, in coordination with Norfund and Scatec Solar, completed a project to increase solar energy capacity in Rwanda. The construction of the first solar-powered farm in East Africa provided jobs to 350 locals, and increased Rwanda's power generation capacity by a full six percent. During its first year in operation the plant produced 15 million kilowatt hours, and brought power to over 15,000 underserved Rwandan residents.

- In December 2014, the Israeli Embassy in Senegal inaugurated a drip-irrigation farm project in the Senegalese city of Fatick. The project is run by Senegalese women and was undertaken at the request of the first lady of Senegal, Marième Faye Sall.

NU Campaign with student
volunteers at SACH, 2010
(David Kramer)

75% of Senagalese citizens are farmers and the Israeli drip irrigation system helps them better regulate their water usage and saves more crops from going bad.

- On World Cancer Day in 2016, 700 women in Kenya were checked for cervical cancer using Enhanced Visual Assessment (EVA) systems donated by MobileODT, a Tel-Aviv based company. The unique technology which only requires a smartphone and internet connection has also been used in over twenty other countries

- With diabetes on the rise in Africa, nurse-educators at Jerusalem's Herzog Hospital lead videoconference classes for healthcare personnel at a Christian hospital in rural Ghana in topics such as diabetes prevention and treatment.

- In July, 2016, Israeli Prime Minister Benjamin Netanyahu dedicated an Israeli-built emergency trauma unit at Kampala's Mulago Hospital in memory of his brother, Yoni, and others killed in the 1976 rescue operation at Entebbe Airport.

And many more. . . .

⤤ Claire Lomus on her way to finishing
the Virgin London Marathon using
Re-Walk suit, 2012. *(ReWalk)*

4 State-of-the-HEART
Life-Saving Technology & Innovation

If an expert says it can't be done, get another expert.
David Ben Gurion

British national Claire Lomus was a professional event horse rider in England until 2007, when she fell off her horse in a freak accident and became paralyzed from the chest down. For five years, Claire was unable to walk, couldn't feel her legs and spent most of her time in a wheelchair.

In January 2012, Claire was given an opportunity to get back on her feet when she was introduced to a unique Israeli technological breakthrough device called ReWalk. ReWalk is a commercial bionic walking assistance system that uses powered leg attachments to enable paraplegics to stand upright, walk and climb stairs. The system is powered by a backpack battery and is controlled by a simple wrist-mounted remote which detects and enhances the user's movements. Designed by Amit Goffer in Yokneam, Israel, and marketed by ReWalk Robotics (originally Argo Medical Technologies,) the device has helped scores of people with physical disabilities worldwide to literally "stand on their feet." The ReWalk and two canes support Claire and the suit senses when she wants to walk and shifts her weight. But it wasn't easy. When she first started using the device, she could take only 30 steps. Every movement was a chore, and because she had no sensations when she was standing, she always feared falling over. That didn't stop her. In April 2012, Lomas set out to participate in the 32nd Virgin London Marathon, a feat which required her completing the 26.2 miles or 42 kilometer (26.2 miles) track in 55,000 steps. She started alongside 35,000 runners and after 17 days, in the shadow of Buckingham Palace, she finished – to the screams of thousands of fans who came out to support her. "It's a moment I'm going to treasure for the rest of my life," she said in a nationally televised, live interview with the BBC after she crossed the finish line. "The support here has been incredible. I didn't expect it here like this. I couldn't believe it when I turned up this morning in the taxi to start, and I thought it was just a busy day in London. Someone told me they're all there for me. I was like, no!"

According to the World Economic Forum's Global Competitiveness Report 2016–2017, Israel ranked second as the most innovative country in the world. The report ranks countries' competitiveness based on 12 categories, including innovation, technological readiness, business sophistication and higher education. Men and women, children and adults of all ages in even the most remote corner of the globe, are affected by Israeli technology, using everyday products such as cell-phones, laptop computers, instant chat communication, cyber-security, navigation, data-analysis and many other innovations. During a visit to Israel, Google's Chairman Eric Schmidt said, "Israel has the most important high-tech center in the world after the US." Israeli research companies, scientists and individual innovators churn out cutting-edge products and services on a continual basis. With just over 7.7 million people, Israel has an estimated 4,800 start-ups. That's one start-up for every 1,604 citizens.

One of the reasons for Israel's innovative progress is that the country, short on natural resources, had to seek creative and alternative sources for much of the country's needs. This is an idea expanded upon in-depth, in a best-selling book titled, "Start-Up Nation," by Saul Singer and Dan Senor. The country's lack of conventional energy sources spurred extensive research and development of alternative energy and Israel continues to develop creative technologies in the solar energy field. In addition to conventional technological innovation, Israeli scientists, high-tech companies and social entrepreneurs are making major contributions in the advancement of agriculture, computer sciences, electronics, genetics, health care, optics and engineering, spearheading STATE OF THE HEART (and not just state-of-the-art) life-saving research and innovations and optimizing technology to improve the quality of life for millions of people worldwide.

In July 2018, news agencies worldwide fixated on the dramatic story of twelve Thai children and their 25-year-old soccer coach who were trapped underground in a flooded cave, as rescuers

worked around-the-clock to save them. The Wild Boars soccer team had been exploring the cave after a practice in the area
when monsoon rains flooded the cave and stranded them alone
for nine days before British cave-divers and Thai Navy seals discovered them. The boys' condition was stable although there was
fear for their physical and mental health if their situation had
continued. What was less-known throughout the team's rescue,
was that Israeli technology became part of the solution. Early rescue efforts were severely hampered by poor communication, as
a result of the four kilometer (2.5 mile) length and depth of the
cave. That's when Israeli company Maxtech Networks stepped in
and donated emergency mobile communication tools worth over
$100,000 each. Maxtech CEO Uzi Hanuni said that Thai authorities had requested assistance from his company, through an Israeli
employee who was based in Thailand. Uzi is a serial Israeli entrepreneur and alumnus of Hebrew University. "We haven't thought
about anything – just to save those kids' lives," he told Israeli press.
As soon as they heard about the mission, employees from the
company gathered all the necessary equipment and hopped on
a plane to Thailand. The systems facilitate communication in areas without reception. "We gave them our devices and they took
them into the cave. This is our Israeli contribution. We did it voluntarily." Maxtech technology does not rely on a cell phone tower
– and their devices were used as a lifeline for the boys to get data
and video-chat with loved ones. MaxTech's devices communicate wirelessly between one another – one link at a time. It's akin
to beacons being lit one hilltop after another, gradually sending a
message in a type of relay. A Maxtech engineer, Yuval Zalmanov
voluntarily included himself within the rescue team in the cave
to help educate them on how to use the communication devices.
Rescuers were racing against the weather, as further monsoon
rains started to raise water levels – flooding the section of the cave

where the boys were stranded. As officials began pumping out water around-the-clock, a decision was made to extract the boys by the divers. The boys were guided around murky passageways in deep water – and many of them did not know how to swim or dive. An ex-Thai navy seal died heroically during the preparation for the rescue as he attempted to supply additional oxygen in the cave. After a three-day rescue operation and to the relief and delight of people worldwide, all 12 boys together with their coach and the rescue personnel that had stayed with them throughout the ordeal, were extracted out alive and unharmed.

Although much of Israel's technological prowess takes place within the commercial sector, there is much innovation taking place in the not-for-profit space, with no other incentive than bettering the quality of people's daily lives.

When Jerusalem born Eli Beer was six years old, he and his brother witnessed a suicide bombing on their way back from school. In the aftermath of the attack, they heard a man yelling for help on the sidewalk but they were so scared they just ran home. This experience instilled within Eli a drive to save lives, so, ten years later, as a teenager and eager to fulfil this mission, he volunteered at a local ambulance service. "In two years of volunteering, however, I never got to save a single life, as we always arrived too late on the scene," he noted. On one occasion, however, his team responded to an emergency call involving a boy choking on a hotdog. There was terrible traffic that day, Eli recalls, and the ambulance tried desperately to get to the scene as quickly as possible. When they finally arrived, they followed procedure and initiated CPR. After a few moments, a doctor, who

www.israel

בשיתוף
הראל
ביטוח ופיננסים

This Ambu

and our chil

Raym

And

Eli Beer, founder of United Hatzalah. *(United Hatzalah)*

lived across the street, came running over to help but told them that it was too late and he declared the boy dead. Eli, heartbroken, realized that the boy died for nothing. "If only the doctor could have been alerted earlier, it would have ended differently." This set him off on what he describes as his life's purpose, to find a better solution. Beer recalled how, as teenagers following the initial bombing incident, he and a group of 15 friends had purchased police transmitters that enabled them to tap into the frequencies of the local ambulance service, so that if anything happened close to their neighborhood, they would be first on the scene. Using this idea as a basis for his new life-saving initiative and following on the success of Hatzalah in New York, in 1996, Beer founded Hatzalah in Jerusalem. The organization has grown considerably over the years and now as United Hatzalah, the volunteers arrive at the scene of an emergency on motorcycle ambulances equipped with an advanced GPS technological application, LifeCompass, which uses crowd-sourcing technology to rally first responders quickly, any time of day or night, across the country. After an emergency call, the organization's GPS application dispatches the call to the closest five medics in the area and they drop whatever they are doing and head towards the scene using the fully-equipped "Ambucycles," supplied by the organization. [LifeCompass was also used by Israeli aid teams in Nepal to map their activities, on the ground and save more lives.] In 2016 alone, the United Hatzalah network of over 3,200 dedicated volunteer medics, provided emergency medical treatment to over 265,000 people, of which 47,000 were life-critical situations with an average response-time of less than three minutes.

In 2007, Eli got a call from two Muslim Arabs living in East Jerusalem, Muhammed Asli and Murad Alyan. Muhammed told him that his 77-year-old father had suffered a heart attack and died in front of his eyes after the ambulance arrived an hour after the distress call. Searching for answers he contacted long-time EMT Murad Alyan. Murad, who knew Eli from their days as ambulance medics, figured that Eli would be the person who could make a difference. They told him that they wanted him to start Hatzalah in their neighborhood. Beer agreed wholeheartedly and with the help of other local volunteers, they started United Hatzalah, East Jerusalem Division. "Hand in hand, Jews and Muslims are working together to save lives. It's not about Jews saving Muslims or Muslims saving Jews, it's just about saving lives," he says.

When Eli's father collapsed from a heart-attack a few years later, the first medic to arrive on the scene and save his father's life was a Muslim Arab from East Jerusalem. "You can imagine how I felt," says Eli. In 2010, Beer received the Social Entrepreneur Award from the Schwab Foundation for Social Entrepreneurship in cooperation with the World Economic Forum of Davos. The award is given to those driving social innovation and transformation in various fields including education, health environment and enterprise development. In 2013, Beer and the organization won the IIE Victor J. Goldberg Prize for Peace in the Middle East and the Jerusalem Prize in 2017. United Hatzalah is also training volunteers in several countries, including the United States, Panama, Argentina, Brazil, Lithuania and India on how to implement its community-based model and technological platform for reaching people in medical distress quickly.

Walking into the offices of TOM Global is an experience in and of itself. The non-profit organization is situated in the heart of WeWork's co-work space in Tel Aviv-Yafo, a local branch of international WeWork, a place by its own standards indicative of the creative entrepreneurship energy that exists in Israel today. TOM Global is an Israeli-founded international movement and network of young innovators and entrepreneurs that brings together strategic thinkers, engineers, designers, and project managers from all walks of life in order to solve unmet social challenges in communities of disabled individuals. The TOM community, with branches in 7 cities worldwide, runs Makeathon events where people with special needs or "need-knowers" are paired with creative teams or "makers" to produce technologically-orientated solutions for practical issues they face on a daily basis. What sets TOM apart from other organizations is that all solutions generated from Makeathon events are "open-sourced" and made available to other people with similar disabilities worldwide. At one such event hosted by a local branch of TOM in Vietnam, Phuong Uyen, a beautiful four-year-old girl with severe cerebral palsy, living in a rural area, was invited to attend with her family. Her limbs are very weak and she's unable to move. She doesn't control her head and neck which contributes to her scoliosis. She can't sit, feed herself, or walk and she is completely dependent on her mother and grandmother. Uyen's family was looking for a chair that would be suitable to support her spine, adjust its size (height and width) for her growth, be flexible for different usage, and which could be made from a material that would provide good air circulation for extended sitting. A wheelchair costs $2000 on average and must be replaced every two years. The family currently only earns $300 a month in Vietnam. Uyen's team of Makers was able to design a special wheelchair that could support her body and expand as she grew.

Another "Makeathon" was held recently in Tel Aviv (an event dubbed TOM: TLV) with the goal of increasing integration and inclusion. "The event was a direct meeting ground for people with special needs and the people with the ability to help solve [their challenges]," TOM Founding Director Arnon Zamir said of the 72-hour program, which produced 25 technological prototypes. Eran Tamir, an employee at IBM Israel, whose son Guy has cerebral palsy, took part in the Tel-Aviv event and described TOM as "a miracle." When Tamir arrived at TOM: TLV, he was swept away by the powerful teams that stayed and worked until midnight or even dawn. The next day, which happened to be Election Day in Israel, Tamir brought Guy to the Tel Aviv event where the makers took time to get to know Guy and to understand his needs. By the end of the day, one group, led by industrial designer Nurit Greenberg, had invented a prototype specifically for Guy. They called it "GidiGuy." Greenberg says her team took it upon themselves to develop a game for children with special needs who would be able to play and interact on an equal level with mainstream youths. Guy, for example, cannot use his hands, so the solution centered on his most easily-moved body part: his head. Greenberg's team, which consisted of a mechanical engineer, economic consultant, architect, and others, designed a game similar to "Simon," using sensors and colored lights. The system recognizes the direction in which Player 1 turns his head. If the player moves right, a red light turns on, while a yellow light is activated by a move to the left, and so on. Player 2 must mimic Player 1. As the players engage, the color sequences get longer and more difficult. Greenberg has been in touch with one of Israel's major hospitals for youths with disabilities to determine if this is something that could be further developed and brought to market.

Other factors that contribute to Israel's technology prowess, as recently discussed by a panel of Israeli innovators at an international convention in Tel-Aviv, include a combination of "intelligence, creativity, productivity and independence as well as their

Vietnamese girl Phuong Uyen during TOM Makeathon. *(Tikun Olam Makers)*

staunch determination to press on in the face of daunting opposition.

After working many years in the plastics industry in Israel, Pablo Kaplan founded Wheelchairs for Hope, an Israeli venture with a goal of impacting the lives of millions of disabled children in developing countries. Of the 65 million people worldwide who require a wheelchair for mobility, approximately 20 million of them do not have access to one, including five million children. Pablo, with over 30 years' experience in the plastics industry, plans to change this and his organization, Wheelchairs of Hope, might do just that. Pablo served as the Vice President of Marketing at Keter Plastics, an Israeli manufacturer of plastic household and garden products, a popular brand in Israel. He set out to create a wheelchair for children that would be affordable as well as comfortable, lightweight, built to last and most importantly would boost the self-esteem of those that used it. He contacted his friend and colleague from his days at Keter, Dr. Amir Ziv Av, now the owner of Ziv Av Engineering Group, and together they developed a lightweight chair – 10 kilograms (22 pounds) as opposed to the standard 15 kilograms – that is able to handle off-road conditions, requires zero maintenance and is simple to assemble. They worked with occupational therapist seating specialists at Jerusalem's Alyn hospital, who provided vital insights for the design of the chair, most important of which was that it would look more like a high chair than a medical device, making it kid-friendly and giving each child a special feeling. The best part of the design is that it can be purchased for only $100. Initial funding for the development of the chair came from his private funds and a grant provided jointly by Israel's Office of the Chief Scientist at the Ministry of Economy and Industry, and the Ministry of Foreign Affairs. The World Health Organization in Switzerland, the Red Cross and UNICEF (To Life Children's Fund) all joined in the project, as well as Nobel laureate Aaron Ciechanover, a personal friend of Kaplan, who has promoted the chair worldwide. Kaplan was joined in the venture by his partner, Chava Rotshtein, and together their vision is to distribute one million chairs over the next decade and to turn the project into a social business venture. The first shipment included 250 wheelchairs for children in institutions in Israel and the Palestinian Authority, with a batch for residents of the refugee camps in Syria soon to follow. And over 600 wheelchairs are being delivered to disabled children in Peru and Tajikistan, funded by a philanthropic foundation and the World Health Organization and other organizations globally are in advanced stages of negotiations for the chair. According to Kaplan, "Mobility empowers access to education and future independence. That is our motto."

In 2014, Forbes magazine listed its pick for the world's top ten most important health tech companies changing the world. More than half of them were Israeli.

- Mobileye, an Advanced Driver Assistance Systems (ADAS) which provides prior warning for incoming road collisions and accidents.
- NaNose, a breathing device which has been proven to detect and differentiate between different kinds of cancers offers up to 95 percent accuracy.
- Babysense breathing monitor, alerting parents of respiratory cessation (apnea) in babies has helped protect more than 600,000 babies from crib deaths around the world.
- Telesofia is a platform that allows doctors to generate personalized videos for their patients describing the proper use

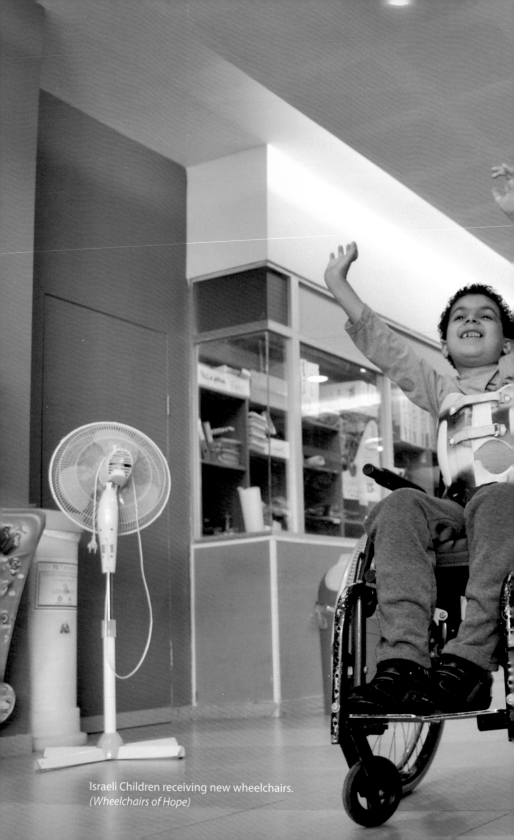

Israeli Children receiving new wheelchairs.
(Wheelchairs of Hope)

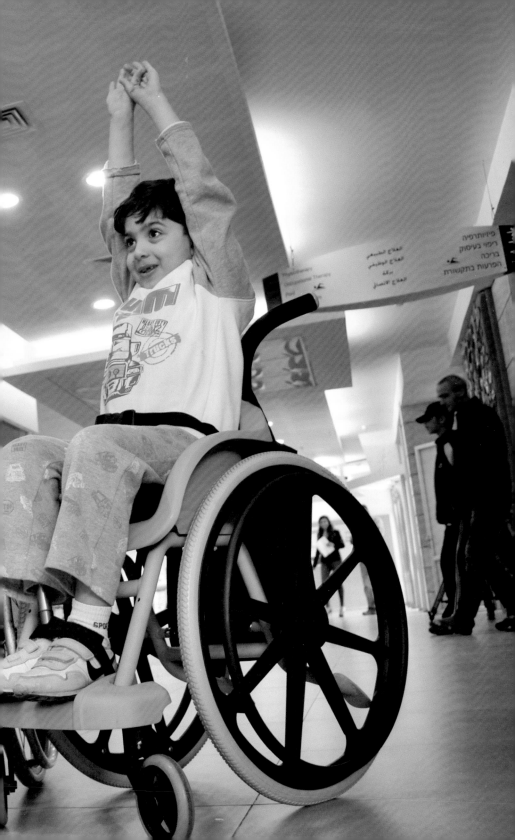

of medication, surgical procedures and discharge instructions.

- HelpAround is a peer-to-peer support application system for diabetes patients, which detects users' locations and connects them to community members nearby so that they can share tips and supplies, and offer each other emotional support.

- uMoove which created face-and-eye-tracking software for mobile devices is now pursuing medical applications that will allow neurological disorders like autism and ADHD to be diagnosed based on eye movement.

Israel's unique security challenges and battlefield experiences have also led the way to many cutting-edge life-saving innovations. Here are a just a few:

- WaterSheer, a water purification system delivers safe drinking water from almost any source including contaminated water, seawater and even urine.

- WoundClot bandages, prevents severe bleeding, through a medically-enhanced highly-absorbent gauze.

- The Emergency Bandage was invented by a former combat medic in the Israel Defense Force. It has a built-in pressure-bar that stops bleeding and has been credited for saving the lives of US servicemen in Iraq, as well as the life of Arizona Congresswoman Gabrielle Giffords.

- The Agilite Instant Harness, the world's smallest Class II rappelling harness, helped save the lives of South African miners trapped underground in 2013.

5 One Human Tissue
Healthcare without Prejudice

Don't look at the vessel, but rather at what it contains.
Ethics of Our Fathers 4:20

At the height of the fighting between Israel and the Hamas terror group in the Gaza Strip, on August 11, 2014, Rev. Raed Abusahliah, a Palestinian Christian pastor and the director of the Catholic humanitarian aid group Caritas Jerusalem, launched a fundraising campaign to collect donations of food, clothing and other vital supplies for the people in Gaza. According to a report of his campaign, covered by USA today, Abusahliah "hoped for generous support from Christians and Muslims eager to help their beleaguered brethren recover from the destruction left by Israel's conflict with Hamas Militants." What Abusahliah didn't anticipate was the outpouring of support from Israeli Jews

89

who, by his own account, constituted about half of the 600–700 donors to the campaign. "I admit that I am somewhat surprised," he said. "Many Jews have also sent us messages of solidarity and offers of everything from baby clothes to blood donations." The polls in Israel may have shown that a vast majority of Jews believed that the Israel Defense Forces had no choice but to put an end to the nearly 4,500 Hamas rocket attacks that had been launched on Israel over the duration of the summer. But according to Angy Shavit, one of the Israelis who promoted Cariatas' campaign through social media, "that doesn't mean we believe the civilians in Gaza are the enemy." Shavit also said that most of the Jewish Israelis who donated to the campaign "don't feel guilty" about Israel's military operation against Hamas. "It's just that when a baby needs diapers you donate diapers."

The Israeli-Palestinian conflict is an ongoing disturbing situation involving many complex factors and as mentioned in the beginning of the book, will not be discussed in detail in this book. What will be said is that several attempts have been made to bring both sides of the conflict together but unfortunately, they have all come to naught. The peace process failures generate much worldwide attention but the many acts of compassion and thoughtfulness for the Palestinians by Israelis, despite the conflict, are hardly known outside of Israel. And this is unfortunate as they take place all the time in all aspects of daily life.

Walking in to the Ein Kerem Campus of Hadassah Ein Kerem Hospital on the outskirts of Jerusalem, one cannot help notice the diversity and vast mix of people that receive treatment and come to heal others within the facility. Labeled an "Island of Coexistence in the Middle-East," the hospital was founded by the Hadassah Woman's Zionist Organization of America and treats over one million people annually from every walk of life in Israel. Hadassah also services the Palestinian population and treats all Palestinian patients that cannot get adequate treatment in areas controlled by the Palestinian Authority, including the West Bank and the Gaza Strip. The hospital is also a global leader in treating mass-casualty incidences including in the aftermath of terror attacks and soldiers wounded in combat and has one of the most advanced emergency trauma-units in the world.

In June 2018, I joined a foreign delegation who visited the hospital. We met with Dr. Abed Khalaileh, a Palestinian surgeon and the Director of the Kidney Transplantation Department at Hadassah. He told our group that on Monday that week, he performed a kidney transplant on an ultra-Orthodox Jewish man from central Jerusalem. On Tuesday, he did the same surgery for a Muslim woman brought to Hadassah from the Gaza Strip and on Wednesday, he did the surgery on a Christian man from Bethlehem, just outside Jerusalem. In his words, "just an average week at Hadassah." The strength of this equality is often tested. On many occasions, as a result of the concentration of terrorist attacks in Jerusalem during the Second Intifada and since the start of the new wave of Palestinian stabbing attacks targeting Israeli Jews, both the victims and the terrorist perpetrators of the incidents arrive simultaneously at the hospital for emergency life-saving treatment. Often they are treated in the same trauma unit only a few beds apart. Doctors and medical personal do not differentiate and provide the necessary treatment to both. This holds true of most hospitals in Israel.

In 2013, Suhila Abd el-Salam, the sister of Hamas' Prime Minister in Gaza, Ismail Haniyah, public enemy number one in

Israel, accompanied her husband for treatment in Israel. He was admitted to Beilinson Hospital in Petach Tikva for immediate medical treatment regarding a serious heart condition.

That same year, the Palestinian Authority Minister of Health, Hani Abdeen, visited Hadassah Hospital, the first visit by a Palestinian minister. Abdeen was accompanied by senior officials from the Palestinian leadership and met with the Director of Hadassah Ein Kerem, Yuval Weiss. In describing the visit, Weiss said, "We relate to patients without regard to nationality and religion. We treat Muslims, Christians, Jews and other nationalities without bias, and 30% of the patients who are children are Palestinians." He went on to say that, "We've begun cooperating with the Palestinians. We now train teams of physicians from the hospital in Beit Jala in Bethlehem, to treat cancer among children. We have about 60 Palestinian medical interns and specialist physicians who will be returning to the Palestinian Authority areas to carry out their work."

Also at a special conference on the topic of humanitarian medicine held at Hadassah Medical Center at Mount Scopus in Jerusalem, November, 2015, Division Medical Officer, Lt. Col. Michael Kassirer said, "The treatment of the Palestinian population is first and foremost a moral and professional obligation for every one of us." In answer to the question of whether they receive the same treatment as Israelis, Kassirer said, "There is no question about it."

An emotional reunion occurred at the Mt. Scopus Hadassah Hospital campus on June 1, 2015, between a Palestinian family and an Israeli army medical officer who had saved the life of their baby son as they crossed the Allenby Bridge from Jordan into Israel the week before. The baby had suffered a cardiac arrest at the crossing and an IDF medical team led by 23-year-old Lt. Ronen Kessler quickly arrived at the scene and performed CPR before the baby was evacuated by helicopter to Hadassah. Kessler and division medical officer Moran Gershoni later visited the family at the hospital. "They were really happy to see us," Kessler said. "Most of the time, the father spoke English. He told us what had happened before they got to the crossing and kept thanking us for what we did. The mother also thanked us and even hugged Gershoni. It was very exciting, but it's not easy to see a boy of six months in such bad shape." "I appreciate everything that IDF soldiers did, and they were praying for my boy," the baby's father said. "They gave him first aid and took him by helicopter to Hadassah, even though he is not Israeli but Palestinian." Gershoni said the army's medical treatment of Palestinians in such cases was unexceptional. "Yesterday we performed CPR on a 16-month-old Palestinian infant with a candy stuck in its throat. On Friday, we were treating an injured Palestinian who was brought to the base gate in an unconscious state," Moran said. "Everyone who needs care is taken care of," Gershoni emphasized. Kessler added that the IDF does not differentiate between "blood and blood;" "That's what we swore to do and what we uphold every day. "The world probably will not see these images," he reflected, stressing that "they represent the real army and our values."

Another Israeli doctor from Hadassah went beyond his "call of duty," when at the height of violent riots that broke out in the city of Nablus, north of Jerusalem, in February 2013, he quietly entered the Palestinian-ruled city, without an army escort, in order to save the life of a young Palestinian man who had been badly injured in the clashes. The doctor in question was Dr. Micah Shamir, a senior Physician at Hadassah, who was made aware of the young man's condition when Palestinian doctors at a Nablus hospital unequipped to save his life reached out for help. "I didn't think twice," said Dr. Shamir. Later, he described the experience: "It was clear we needed to save this young man. But entering Shechem (Nablus) was not pleasant, and there were moments of real fear." While the rescue operation was sanctioned by the Palestinian mayor of Shechem, had any of the local terror groups decided to attack or abduct the Israeli doctor, they could have easily done so. "It was extremely dangerous," Dr. Shamir recalled. Ultimately, the mission was a success, and the young Palestinian man was secreted out of Nablus and transferred to the hospital in Jerusalem.

On April 10, 2019 I met with Audrey Gross who works in the Public Affairs department of Shaare Zedek Hospital ("Gates of Righteousness") in Jerusalem. Shaare Zedek is today the city's fastest growing hospital and the only major medical facility in the city's center. Shaare Zedek is well known internationally for its emergency response systems which have been extensively developed and sadly put to the ultimate test due to the area's ongoing battle with terrorism. This includes an extensive decontamination system capable of responding to terrorist attacks involving chemical warfare. Shaare Zedek acts as the on-call facility for the entire Jerusalem area responsible to respond in the event of such attacks.

During our discussion, Audrey told me how the hospital, like many of Israel's major hospitals, treats thousands of Palestinian and Arab patients every year and when I asked if she knows the exact number, she answered it doesn't matter since the hospital treats every patient the same regardless of their origin, religion or ethnicity. She also told me the following story, illustrating the type of care that one confronts every day in the hospital.

Two volunteers from abroad had come to distribute gifts at the hospital to newborn babies and their families. Audrey accompanied them to the NICU (Neonatal Intensive Care Unit). They approached a young Arab woman, wearing a hijab on her head and tightly holding her newborn child. Initially the young mother ignored the two volunteers until they started speaking to her in their native English tongue and she responded saying that she too was born in America before her parents sent her to Israel to get married. They spoke for a while and then parted ways leaving the new mother a few gifts for her child. A few months later as Audrey walked past the NICU, the same Arab woman spotted her, ran up to her and gave her a big hug. She proceeded to tell Audrey her story. Tragically, the day they had first met in the ward, was the day that her baby, suffering from a terminal illness, had died. Before the birth doctors gave the unborn child a zero percent chance of survival. Still, the mother decided to go ahead with the pregnancy, motivated by the feeling that there was a lesson to be learned from the experience, no matter how difficult it would be. She described her amazement by the extent to which the Israeli doctors tirelessly worked to save her Arab child, which totally contradicted what she had learned and understood of Israel's attitude towards their Arab neighbors. Noticing Audrey's surprise at seeing her in the NICU, the young mother opened her bag revealing gifts she had bought to distribute to other sick kids and their families in the ward. She explained that from the moment she met the hospital staff, she was treated like any other expectant mother, which took her mind off of the suffering she was dealing with, and now she wished to show the same kindness and compassion that she received. She described her volunteer activities with an organization called "First Hug," whose volunteers come and spend time applying the kangaroo method, a technique of newborn care where babies are kept chest-to-chest and skin-to-skin. These are newborn babies that have been abandoned or do not receive enough skin-to-skin contact with their families for various reasons. Shortly after seeing Audrey, the bereaved mother penned the following letter to the staff of the NICU:

"It is with a heavy heart that I'm writing you this thank you note. As you know my precious baby girl passed away six days before she turned a month old. Although we were all prepared for her not to live a long life, we definitely were not expecting it to be this short, especially with the new diagnosis we had been given. Yet, such is life. A constant reminder of things we can and cannot control. Countless times I was told to abort while pregnant, that her life expectancy was very short, if anything at all. For whatever reason, I held on to the hope that whatever was meant to come from her life, no matter how short, would be for good. And good it was indeed. I was shown a generosity and kindness that I can't properly express in words. Inside Shaare Zedek, there was no Palestinian/Israeli struggle. You all did your jobs like angels sent from God. My child was not shown any less love than the sweet Jewish boy next to her. You smiled and loved my daughter like any other child being cared for. You all have restored my belief in the goodness of humanity; we are all working for the betterment of our children. Our daughter was named according to the

Muslim and Jewish doctors working
side by side at NICU, Shaare Zedek
Hospital.
(*Shaare Zedek Hospital*)

Arabic word for faith, and it's exactly what gives meaning to our lives. Even in the darkest days, it's our belief in faith that things will get better, that we can handle our sorrows, and overcome the obstacles we face. If I could thank each of you individually, trust me that I would. I grew so accustomed to seeing you all more than my own family. You will never fully know the appreciation I have for the job that you do. There is a bond that grows between you all and the parents in the NICU, no doubt about it. So if I happen to see you around sometime, don't be surprised if I stop you to say hello! After all, you were such a huge part of my life and for that I will forever be grateful. Once again, thank you from the bottom of my heart for the kindness you not only showed me, my husband, and my family . . . but for your unrelenting support and encouragement you gave to my precious baby girl, Faith.

Sincerely yours,
N.N."

In Israel, interactions take place constantly between people from different walks of life, shattering preconceived perceptions of who and what Israelis, of all types, are really all about. These incidents serve to challenge our general ability to look beyond what we hear from others about events and people in our everyday lives and draw our own conclusions.

In August, 2014, Arab-Israeli Ziad Dawiyat was on duty with Magen David Ambulance Service when a Palestinian terrorist drove his car into a crowd waiting at a Jerusalem light rail station, killing an Ecuadorian tourist as well as Hanna and Shmuel Braun's three-month-old baby. Dawiyat, a senior MDA paramedic, was

Medic Ziad Dawiyat. *(MDA Spokesperson)*

one of the first emergency personnel on the scene and he trans-
ported the critically injured Braun to the hospital in his ambulance. Ten months later, on August 10th, 2015, Hannah Braun
went into labor with the couple's second child. With the con-
tractions coming frequently and fiercely, her husband, Shmuel,
called an ambulance, and as it happened, it was Dawiyat and his
team that were dispatched to the ultra-Orthodox couple's home in
Jerusalem. When they arrived, Dawiyat checked Hannah's condition and decided that her labor had progressed too far for her to
be moved to a hospital and he proceeded to deliver the baby in the
apartment. It wasn't until after the delivery when both mother and
baby were doing fine that a shocked Hannah recognized Dawiyat.
"She thanked me, and while I was preparing to give her an IV, the
husband hugged and kissed me. It was very emotional," Dawiyat
said in a statement put out by MDA. "I didn't know what to do
or say – to wish them congratulations or give them my condo-
lences," Dawiyat said. "I was very moved so I just wished them

'mazel tov' and a long and peaceful life. I would never have imagined even in my dreams that I would be able to come full circle with the Brauns, but it's a small world," he added.

One year earlier, in August 2013, Haitham Azloni, an Arab resident of East Jerusalem, was sitting next to his stall in the Arab bazaar near the Old City's Damascus Gate when his heart stopped beating following his attempts to fix an electric short. He had been electrocuted and was sprawled on the floor, seemingly dead. Haim Attias, a resident of Mitzpe Yericho – located just northeast of Jerusalem and 15 minutes from the Dead Sea – and a certified medic, was walking through the bazaar just then and when he noticed Azloni lying on the ground, he rushed to his assistance. After a long attempt to resuscitate him, Azloni's heart rate was restored and stabilized. He was taken by ambulance to the hospital where he was treated and released after several days. A week later Azloni invited Attias to his home in the Old City's Muslim Quarter. When Azloni awoke in the hospital on the day of the incident, he told his brother the following: "No one came to help me, none of the brothers, no Arabs. Only one Orthodox Jewish man came to help me. I want to meet the man that saved me." Finding Attias was not difficult to do. "I'm hard to forget," Attias noted smiling and pointed to his big crocheted skullcap, sidelocks and beard. Attias was welcomed by Azloni to his home with a hug and a traditional kiss on both cheeks. While sitting together on the couch, one of Azloni's young children came to sit between them, and he later high-fived the Jewish guest. "Thank him (gesturing to Attias) and thank God, or I would not be here." Attias explained that when it came to helping others, nationalities and religious affiliation never stand in his way. "When I arrive at a scene, I don't think about the politics; all I think about is saving lives. It's not a matter of peace or no peace. I'm certain that this is what God expects from me."

Yuval Roth, founder of On The Road To Recovery. *(On The Road To Recovery)*

In 1993, Yuval Roth's brother Udi was kidnapped and killed by members of Hamas. Roth searched for a way to recover from his personal tragedy and channel his anger into peace. "I heard an interview on Israeli radio with a man who lost his son in the same way that I lost my brother," Roth said. "After the interview, I spoke to him and he told me about an idea he had to establish some sort of group to encourage dialogue between bereaved families from both sides, Israelis and Palestinians." Yuval joined the group, called Parents Circle – Families Forum, and discovered that both Palestinians and Israelis shared the same concern – how to transport the sick or injured to Israeli health-care facilities in good time. "Medical facilities are limited in the Palestinian controlled areas of the West Bank and it's also expensive for many Palestinians to make the trip to Israeli hospitals," Roth said. Roth went beyond the original intent of Parents Circle. In 2006, he established a nonprofit organization, called Derech Hachlama ("On the Road to Recovery") to help the situation. The first call for help was over four years ago. As word of Roth's generosity spread, transportation demands grew, and Roth began to recruit his friends as driver-volunteers. Today, Roth's group has grown to 200 volunteers. Transport coordination efforts are run entirely by Roth, who puts in many hours pinpointing the location of volunteers and Palestinian families. Each volunteer maintains his or her own vehicle, but Roth helps cover gasoline costs with money he receives from anonymous donors. Even though differences exist, including the obvious language barriers, Roth believes that the program helps Israelis and Palestinians understand and respect each other. "When we are on our way to pick up the sick kids, the (Palestinian and Israeli) checkpoint managers help us a lot," Roth said. "It makes our life and their life a lot easier. I think Palestinian families trust me also because I'm coming as one of them. I feel like they are my family or my friends." Roth's group has driven an estimated 90,000 kilometers (56,000 miles) in 2010 alone. He said they have helped hundreds of Palestinians get access to health care. "I lost my brother, but I didn't lose my head," Roth said. "This activity gives me an essence for life. I have learned that the price of the conflict is a lot more than the price of making peace. We are all human beings."

Today, Hamas is the official governing body in the Gaza Strip and is an internationally recognized Islamic terror organization avowedly committed to the destruction of Israel. Israel withdrew completely from the Gaza Strip in 2005. Hamas seized power in the enclave in 2007. Since then, Hamas has fired over 14,000 rockets and fought three wars with Israel. In order to prevent Hamas from importing weapons or transferring military equipment of any kind into Gaza, Israel together with Egypt, has maintained a blockade over the seaside territory along the Strip.

Despite these restrictions, Israel maintains an ongoing humanitarian corridor for the transfer of perishable and fresh goods, building materials and humanitarian aid to the population of Gaza via a checkpoint on the Israeli side of the bor-

Trucks transporting goods through Israel into Gaza. *(Wikipedia)*

der. This conduit is used by internationally recognized organizations including from Israel and the Red Cross. Besides material goods, Gazans are allowed to cross the border into Israel to
enjoy the benefits of Israel's medical services. A report published
in 2013 by Israel's Coordinator of Government Activities in the
Territories Unit (COGAT) shows that 219,464 Palestinian patients
received medical treatment in Israeli hospitals during 2012. Of
them, 21,270 were children, who were escorted by family members. And in 2015, over 190,000 Palestinians received medical
treatment in Israel, with a companion.

Marianne of Gothenburg, a large Swedish boat, with three other
vessels following closely behind, set sail from Crete toward the
Gaza Strip in April 2015. Their mission was "to bring vital humanitarian supplies to the people of Gaza and protest the Israeli naval
blockade on the Gaza enclave." The ship was carrying 47 participants including Israeli Arab MK Bassel Ghattas and ex-Tunisian
president, Moncef Marzouki. Just days before, Marzouki's country had been hit by one of the worst terror attacks in its history
when a lone ISIS supporter, Seifeddine Rezgui, gunned down 38
tourists on a holiday resort beach in broad daylight. As it happened, a film crew from Channel 2 news in Israel, had permission to document the event. This was the third event of its kind
following the incident of the 'Gaza Freedom Flotilla' which was
organized by the Free Gaza Movement and had taken place five
years before in May 2010. At that time, the flotilla was requested to
stop its approach and it refused to do so. When Israeli naval com-

mandos caught up with it and boarded the ship where Turkish Foundation for Human Rights and Freedoms and Humanitarian Relief (İHH) representatives were standing, an angry mob attacked them with knives and poles and dragged an IDF soldier into the lower deck of the boat. The event resulted in the death of nine people and was followed by large international condemnation of Israel and the straining of relations between Turkey and Israel, which took years to repair. This time, Israel made it clear to those on the Swedish ship that it was in violation of its territorial borders and international laws and that it would stop the boat upon its arrival. As the boats approached Israeli waters, three of the four vessels turned around and left the Swedish boat to continue on its own. The event ended without incident. Israel's navy intercepted and boarded the ship and then escorted it to Ashdod port where its contents were checked and its passengers deported from the country. In contrast to the statements of the people on board the ship, The Washington Post reported that, "Only two cardboard boxes of humanitarian aid were found on the ship, one carrying a single solar panel and the other a small nebulizer machine. What was all the fuss about?" The Israeli Prime Minister's office released a statement in response to the incident pointing out that Israeli humanitarian aid to the population of Gaza, had in the past year amounted to "500,000 times more than that of the first Flotilla ship and that there was no need for ships coming to the aid of the Gazans. 500 truckloads of humanitarian aid pass into the Strip every day, from Israel."

The Hamas leadership is fully aware of the value the State of Israel places on an individual life. At the outbreak of the Gaza War in 2014, Hamas TV decided to broadcast a statement by former Hamas Prime Minister Ismail Haniyeh made several years earlier. "We love death like our enemies love life! We love martyrdom, the way in which Hamas leaders died." Several months after the war, Amal Haniyeh, the granddaughter of the same Hamas leader, Ismail Haniyeh, was hospitalized in Israel in critical condition and her life was saved by Israeli doctors.

6 Humanity in Arms
A Military Code of Ethics

*If you can't get up for an old woman on the bus, you can't
be an officer in the IDF.*
> Lt. Gen. (res.) Moshe Ya'alon, Chief of Staff,
> Israel Defense Force, 2001–2005

On my final night of basic training in the Israeli
army, June 14, 2002, I was part of an army unit made up of 60
soldiers who, laden with 30 kilograms (66 pounds) of equipment
and ammunition on our backs, set off on a grueling 70-kilometer
(43-mile) hike along the hilly Negev desert in the southern part
of Israel. This maneuver was the climax of almost five months of
basic training and at the end of it we were to receive our unit's
beret. It was the height of the Second Intifada, and due to security precautions, all army hiking routes had been redirected to the

Negev desert in order to avoid proximity to the nearby Palestinian villages and cities. Approximately fifteen kilometers into the hike as the sun was setting, we passed a construction site with large Caterpillar diggers parked on the side. With the exception of one soldier at the back of the group, no one noticed that one of the trucks had turned on its engine and was making its way in the direction we were walking.

The driver of the digger positioned his machine alongside the two rows of soldiers, lifted the vehicle's large spade, and as he shouted, "Allahu Akbar," (God is great) he put his foot on the gas pedal and sped full-throttle toward us, intent on killing as many soldiers as he could. With the vehicle closing in on us, chaos ensued, with soldiers running in every direction to get out harm's way. Much to our consternation, our commander issued an order forbidding us from firing even one bullet. He later explained that he did not feel at the time that our lives were "enough" in danger. The driver of the Caterpillar continued approaching a group of soldiers who managed to get out of the way in time. Then he reversed, lined up again and attempted to trample a different group. This time he came very close. But our orders not to shoot were clear so all we could do was to run for our lives.

Eventually, defying the commander's orders, Itzik, a small kibbutznik from the north of Israel, decided he had seen enough. He picked up a rock, ran right up to the side of the digger and threw the rock hard at the driver, striking him in the head. The driver fell out the digger and lay unconscious on the ground. The vehicle continued its own for about 20 meters (65 feet) and then came to a halt. We were all relieved that the incident had come to an end without any injuries to our group but many of us were upset at the orders we had received which we felt had not allowed us to defend ourselves but had instead put our lives in danger. I will never forget, however, what happened next. As the commotion began to abate, I looked up and saw our unit's medic, Eyal Banin, kneeling on the ground at the terrorist's side, administering first aid. The incongruity of the moment was blatantly apparent. Here was an Israeli soldier saving the life of someone who had just tried to murder him and his friends. Eyal didn't hesitate in his work, determined to save the life of the injured man. He stopped the bleeding, cleaned the wound and applied the necessary bandages. He poured him some water and slowly brought him back to life. We all waited until the ambulance and police arrived and then continued our march into the night.

In 2006, on the final day of his annual reserve duty, Eyal was killed by Hezbollah terrorists in a cross border ambush, in which two other soldiers, Ehud Goldwasser and Eldad Regev, were killed and their bodies abducted. The event shook the country and triggered the start of the second Lebanon War. Staff Sergeant Eyal Banin, an only child, from the southern Israeli city of Beersheba, had strived desperately to become a combat soldier, so he could contribute to the defense of his country, a move at odds with the IDF directive that requires an only child to get special parental permission before enlisting. Eyal already had plans to move to Jerusalem with friends and study at Hebrew University when his life was so tragically cut short. He was a dear friend.

The challenge of Israel's obligation to defend its own citizens, while at the same time upholding the highest standards of morality was best put by the IDF's 19th Chief of Staff, Gabi Ashkenazi, in a letter addressed to IDF soldiers before the Jewish holiday of Passover, 2009: "The ethos of the IDF is based on combining our strength with our righteousness; on the one hand, our need to hold a sword of deterrence against those who threaten to destroy us, and on the other hand, our continuous effort to establish peace. We fulfill this task with determination, while preserving our morality as Jews, as Israelis and as followers of the 'Spirit of the IDF' [the IDF's ethical code]".

"The IDF's Ethical Code is a document representing the values and responsibilities shaping the mode of action applied by all IDF soldiers and units which is studied and analyzed by soldiers and their commanders during basic training. This ethical code is customarily hung in a frame in every commander's office as a constant reminder of the IDF's values and guidelines.

Israel has learned to take threats seriously and is at the forefront of the global fight against terror, as it faces hostilities and attacks from fundamentalist terror organizations on a continuous basis. There are currently no less than ten terrorist organizations operating within and around Israel's borders, including Hamas, Hezbollah, the Al-Aqsa Martyrs Brigade and now ISIS. Israel, however, still considers the fundamentalist Iranian regime as its greatest threat. Tehran not only sponsors weapons, training and funding to some of the above-mentioned terrorist groups but by harboring nuclear aspirations, constantly threatens to wipe Israel off the map. In 2001, Iranian spiritual leader, Ayatollah Ali Khamenei announced that "It is the mission of the Islamic Republic of Iran *to erase Israel* from the map of the region." In 2012, he said, "The Zionist regime is a cancerous tumor and it will be removed."

Article seven of the Hamas Charter, states that "The Day of Judgment will not come about until Muslims fight the Jews (killing the Jews), when the Jew will hide behind stones and trees. The stones and trees will say O Muslims, there is a Jew behind me, come and kill him."

The war on terror is a complex and difficult necessity and this is due to the ideological nature and cynical tactics employed by the terrorists themselves. The way that IDF soldiers operate in these extreme situations deserves examination, as the morality and high ethical standards to which they abide is unparalleled anywhere else in the world.

In the Gaza war of 2014, during an operational mission in the Shejaiya neighborhood, Israeli soldiers found a Hamas "doctrine manual" which documented how the terror group urged its fighters to embed themselves among civilians in hopes that the "IDF will kill civilians." Members of Hamas are acutely aware of the IDF's rules of engagement and the Israeli fighting ethic – to do the utmost to avoid civilian casualties – and they take advantage of this moral stance by consistently using the inhuman tactic of embedding its military infrastructures and fighters within their civilian population, inviting an Israeli response that inflicts civilian deaths and destruction. Despite international confirmation of this ruse, it inevitably triggers global condemnation of Israel and sympathy for Hamas's cause. It is a well-known fact that before attacking terrorist infrastructure and targets in civilian neighborhoods, the IDF drops *warning leaflets*, calls the civilians by phone to notify them to evacuate and institutes "roof knockings," on buildings slated to be attacked, giving residents time to leave. During Operation Cast Lead, 2008–2009, the IDF dropped more than 2,250,000 leaflets during the fighting and made personal telephone warnings to more than 165,000 Gaza residents. On a fact-finding mission into the Gaza war in 2014, professor of international law, Willy Stern of Vanderbilt Law School reflected, "It was abundantly clear that IDF commanders had gone beyond any mandates that international law requires to avoid civilian casualties."

Captain Dor is a 26-year-old Air Force pilot from Tel Aviv who serves in the 106th Squadron in the Israeli Air Force. He began his service eight years ago and while taking a rare break from the fighting between Israel and Hamas, during Operation Protective Edge in Gaza in 2014, shared his "bird-eye" testimony of events:

> For me on a personal level, it was very hard bombing at night when you're waiting for clearance to strike and you see rockets coming out of Gaza. At night you see them very clearly. They light up the sky. And you realize that now in Tel Aviv and Ashdod and Sderot, people are running to bomb shelters. It's almost surreal to see these rockets close up, lighting up the sky in front of you, just as your friends and family are running to bomb shelters. You know that this rocket launcher is your target but you can't attack because you have to wait for clearance to make sure that there are no civilians in the area where the rocket is being launched. Only once you know your target is clear, and there are no civilians nearby, then that is the time to strike. I saw several occasions where Gazans ran to the roof of a building that had been warned of an imminent strike, or people simply remaining where they were and that's the biggest of all the dilemmas we face. . . . Every strike mission I went on had those dilemmas. . . . Many times as a pilot you're very close to releasing a bomb and sometimes with five seconds or three seconds to launch, you abort the mission because there are civilians in the vicinity and you're not willing to take those risks. Sometimes the civilians aren't exactly in the target

but they're close enough that you feel that if you attack they could get hurt. So sometimes you come back for landing with all your bombs, because you're waiting two hours and still the target wasn't clear. About 20 to 30 percent of the targets I was assigned to were aborted for that reason. I saw targets in schoolyards, in parks next to swings, and you realize that Hamas takes the most innocent place, like next to a swing, and builds a rocket launcher there. In his mind, the Israeli Air Force won't attack it because there's a good chance there will be children nearby. And for Hamas, when children are killed, it is considered a great success. In this way, they manage to force the Israelis to harm innocent children "by accident." We do everything in our power to avoid it, which is a paradox. You do everything in your power to make the Gaza civilians safe, and Hamas does everything in its power to keep civilians in danger.

Sergeant Gedaliah F., a 20-year-old from Raanana and a sniper in the Nachal Brigade, went into Gaza on the first day of the ground operation. Over the phone he shared the following account:

"I'm a sniper in my unit and we were shot at from a school about 250 meters (800 feet) away. I couldn't see into the school because the windows were tinted. And it just puts you in this very hard position. You don't want to shoot at a school. What if there are kids there? You can't just shoot if you don't see what you're shooting at. It's a school. But on the other hand, you're being shot at by an enemy sniper. It really hits two ends of the spectrum and you really don't know what to do. And it was like that throughout the entire war. We were in Beit Hanoun. I'm almost 100 percent sure that it was an UNRWA school. People in my unit remember it hav-

Israeli soldier holds Hamas
poster in Gaza, 2014.
(Israel Defense Forces)

ing a UN flag. If I had to guess, it was. It was a big beautiful white building with blue frames in the middle of a village of grey buildings with no rooftops. [The IDF confirmed that this incident took place at an UNRWA school.] There were tons of buildings that were higher than that school. He [the terrorist] clearly chose that spot not because it was higher up. He knew the consequences of us shooting there and he tried to use that against us."

The cynical tactics of Hamas were also evident during protests along the Israeli-Gaza security fence in 2018, dubbed, the "Great March of Return," which are still ongoing at the time of writing this book. The protests, largely portrayed by international media as "peaceful protests" are nothing less than a *smokescreen* to cover a deliberately engineered military strategy by Hamas, to fatally undermine Israel.

Colonel Richard Kemp – a former commander of British forces in Afghanistan and a leading international expert on counter-terrorism strategy said during the protests that, "In reality these demonstrations are far from peaceful but are carefully planned and orchestrated tactical operations by a terrorist organization intending to break through the border of a sovereign state and commit mass murder in the communities beyond, using their own civilians as cover."

While the media outcry focuses on the fact that a large number of the Palestinian protestors have been killed – over 200 so far – the majority of them were identified by Hamas themselves, as "active combatants" and members of their organization. What the press ignored was that behind the "peaceful protestors," Hamas militants, dressed in civilian clothing, fired weapons at Israeli soldiers, planted explosives along the security fence, burned tires and attempted to break-through the fence. In addition thousands of helium balloons and kites, attached with burning instruments and explosives were launched by Hamas, igniting fires and setting alight to thousands of acres of agricultural land within Israel, with damages in the millions of dollars. In one incident, four Israeli soldiers were severely wounded when they attempted to remove a Palestinian flag placed along the fence the day before, during one of the protests. As soon as the soldiers handled the flag a device placed below the flag detonated and caused serious injuries to the soldiers.

Israel has been bringing this unacceptable situation for years to the UN and to major news outlets all of which have turned a blind eye to the fact. Thankfully, this deception is finally being acknowledged: United Nations Office for the Coordination of Humanitarian Affairs director, John Ging, reported to CBC News on July 30, 2014 during the fighting in Gaza. "Yes, the armed groups [in Gaza] are firing their rockets into Israel from the vicinity of UN facilities and residential areas, absolutely." William Booth of the Washington Post reported during one temporary ceasefire in Gaza 2014, that he saw a "group of men" at a mosque in northern Gaza. They said they had returned to clean up glass from shattered windows. "But they could be seen moving small rockets into the mosque," Booth wrote. He also reported that Shifa Hospital in Gaza City had, "become a de facto headquarters for Hamas leaders, who can be seen in the hallways and offices." During the same battle, Wall Street Journal reporter Nick Casey tweeted an image of a Hamas spokesman giving an interview at a Gaza hospital with sounds of the shelling clearly heard in the background. "You have to wonder . . . how patients at Shifa Hospital feel as Hamas uses it as a safe place to show the media." The tweet was later deleted. According to Middle East analyst Matthew Levitt, Hamas had been planting weapons in areas inhabited by vulnerable residents for a long time. "It happens in schools," he wrote in Middle East Quarterly. "Hamas has buried caches of arms and explosives under its own kindergarten playgrounds. . . ."

The IDF and its soldiers are not perfect and like all conflicts mistakes resulting from intelligence and operational errors are made. The IDF thoroughly investigates every incident of misconduct and brings anyone who has mistreated innocent civilians or acted out of line according to the IDF ethical code to trial. Following Operation Cast Lead, the United Nations Human Rights Council set up an investigation into alleged Israeli war crimes, headed by South African judge Richard Goldstone. The findings came to be known as the "Goldstone Report." The initial inquiry, published throughout worldwide media, accused Israel of, "using disproportionate force, deliberately targeting civilians and destroying civilian infrastructure, and using people as human shields." It did, however, also accuse Hamas of deliberately targeting civilians and trying to spread terror through its rocket attacks. However, almost two years later, following an additional report by a separate U.N.

committee of independent experts, Richard Goldstone's reversed his conclusion in an op-ed piece published in The Washington Post, April 1, 2011. "We know a lot more today about what happened in the Gaza war," Goldstone admitted. "If I had known then what I know now, the Goldstone Report would have been a different document." Those investigations, he said, indicate that, "civilians were not intentionally targeted as a matter of policy." Hamas, by contrast, "has not carried out any investigations, according to the follow-up committee." In the article Goldstone says that the UN report recognized and accepted the findings of 400 IDF investigations into alleged allegations. Of the many incidents Goldstone investigated, one of the most serious attacks was the killing of 29 members of the al-Simouni family by Israeli shelling of their home. He wrote that Israel's own investigation admitted the occurrence and had concluded that the shelling was apparently the result of an Israeli commander's mistaken analysis of a drone image and that the officer was being investigated.

The IDF ethical code, not only defines ethical behavior expected of soldiers in their conduct toward the *enemy* and its civilian population but a major part of the document outlines values and principles expected of Israeli soldiers, in their interaction with their comrades-in-arms. Years of war and conflict between Israel and its Arab neighbors, have resulted in infinitive acts of heroism and bravery where Israeli soldiers and civilians, facing the most unimaginable circumstances, have placed their own lives on the line to protect their comrades, families, friends and country. Here are just two examples:

Israeli soldier rescues Lebanese woman near the Israel-Lebanese border, 2010.
(Israel Defense Forces.)

In the third week of the Second Lebanon War, in July 2006, as fighting raged between Israel and the Lebanese-based Hezbollah terror group, Maj. Roi Klein, a highly-decorated deputy commander of the 51st Battalion of the Golani Brigade, led his men into a building in the center of the Lebanese village of Bint Jbeil. During the attempt to take the structure, the team's scouts got caught in an olive grove surrounded by stone walls and the area quickly turned into a fierce battle – the most difficult of the war – against Hezbollah terrorists. The troops were attacked from behind, from the sides, with heavy fire, without being able to see the enemy. The Golani soldiers waged a heroic fight for a full 11 hours. During the fighting a hand-grenade was lobbed into the building where Klein and his soldiers were standing. Klein instantly dived on the grenade to save his fellow soldiers. In the last seconds of his life, Roi mustered the strength to shout "Shema Yisrael" the prayer that Jews have recited for centuries, declaring belief in God and in the World to Come; the prayer that so many Jewish martyrs throughout the generations cried out as they were being led to their deaths. With his last remaining strength he reported his own death through the radio: "Klein is dead," he said over military radio and handed the device to another officer, who took over the command of the force. At the end of the battle eight IDF fighters and commanders were killed and 25 were wounded. The Israeli soldiers were ultimately victorious and the 51st Battalion and 17 of its soldiers were awarded decorations for their bravery.

During the fighting in Gaza in 2014, Hamas terrorists emerged from a tunnel shaft in the vicinity of a group of Israeli soldiers.

One of the terrorists proceeded to detonate himself, killing three IDF soldiers in the process and kidnapping the body of one of them, Lt. Hadar Goldin, dragging him down the same tunnel from where these terrorists had emerged. Believing that Hadar might still be alive, Lt. Eitan, one of Hadar's good friends along with three soldiers under his command, chased after the terrorists into the pitch-dark tunnel for hundreds of meters, fully aware of a possible ambush and without any prior knowledge as to where they were going or how to get back. "I went four meters (13 feet) down into the tunnel when it began to collapse," recalled Eitan. "I could hardly see anything; and stones were obscuring the light. I returned to the surface, took my equipment, my helmet and gun, and went back into the tunnel with my soldiers." Before entering the tunnel, he told his commander, "If I'm not back in 5 minutes, I'm dead." As a result of the pursuit, Eitan and his team found evidence that later helped the military rabbinate (religious authority) draw the conclusion that Goldin had been killed before his body was taken. In an emotional encounter at the Goldin family house that week, Eitan came to present the family with belongings of their son and speak to his family. Israel's President Reuven Rivlin was paying a *shiva* (mourning) call at the time and spoke to Eitan. "You may take your act of heroism for granted, but it gives us a lot of hope," the president told him. "Your decision is awe-inspiring. Your soldiers are heroes on a personal level, and also on a national and moral level."

As of October 2019, Hadar Goldin's body has still not been returned by Hamas, in violation of international law as defined by the Geneva Convention.

Israeli soldier teaching
emergency drill to
Israeli-Arab students.
(Israel Defense Forces)

7 Turning Tragedy Around

As a people, our monuments never commemorate victories. They commemorate the names of the fallen. We don't need the Arc de Triomphe; we have Masada, Tel-Hai, and the Warsaw Ghetto – where the battle was lost, but the war of Jewish existence was won.
David Elazar – IDF Chief of Staff, 1972–1974

The state of Israel today is a bustling developed country with a thriving economy, tourism and cultural scene comparable with many other modern countries worldwide. It's quite remarkable to see how far the country has come in just over 70 years. However, this reality did not come easy and there has been a tremendous amount of sacrifice and suffering along the way. In fact, throughout history, adversity has always been a central re-

...ummer made out of Qassam ...kets in Sderot, 2015. *(David ...amer)*

ality of Jewish life and Jewish tradition places great significance on remembering our national tragedies together with our celebrations. One explanation for this is that in order to truly appreciate something one needs to understand the difficult journey that made it possible. There is probably no better occasion to witness this concept than on Israel's annual Independence Day, when Israelis countrywide celebrate the recognition of Israel as a state by hosting barbeques, parties and public festivities. The "happiest day in Israel" is also, however, a bittersweet moment, as the day is preceded by Israel's Remembrance Day for fallen soldiers and victims of terrorism. On this day, special ceremonies are held in schools, communities, private homes, businesses and institutions telling the stories of Israel's fallen and a two-minute moment of silence is held nationwide while a siren sounds to pay respect.

War and terrorism have plagued Israel from even before its founding. The number of fallen soldiers and victims of terror in Israel between the years 1860 and 2018 stands at 26,780. The trauma and suffering from terror attacks has left a huge toll on Israeli society and the survivors, friends and family of victims often spend a life-time recovering and rehabilitating from the events. There are also thousands of Arabs that have lost their lives during this region's bitter never-ending conflicts. The way each person responds to these global incidents is unique and some in Israel have, remarkably, turned their personal tragedies and nightmares into meaningful and beneficial applications that have assisted others going through similar experiences.

On April 19, 2018, the Israel Prize, recognizing Israeli citizens who have "achieved excellence in their fields" was awarded to Miriam Peretz for her work in youth education throughout the country. Peretz, lost two of her sons in combat. In 1998, her oldest son, Uriel, was killed while serving in Lebanon. 12 years later in 2010, her other son, Eliraz, was killed on the Gaza border. Both served in the elite Sayeret Golani unit. At the Prize awards ceremony in Jerusalem which took place on Independence Day, Peretz spoke on behalf of all the Israel Prize laureates:

"I am proud to be part of a group that chose to engage in education, out of the belief that this is the way to breach the walls of ignorance and inadequacy, and out of the understanding that education opens opportunities for self-fulfillment, as it had for me.

"Ladies and gentlemen, I stand humbly before my colleagues, honorable people who created, wrote, studies and invented, people of vision, creation and faith. I am not worthy, I don't have a creation. I can't point to a revelation I made or a formula I cracked. I have a *heart* that was broken three times with terrible announcements: The loss of my eldest son Uriel in battle in Lebanon, the death of my partner Eliezer due to a broken heart, and the loss of my second son in battle in Gaza," she recalled. "With that heart I came to my nation and in simple words, in the language of a broken heart, I spoke of this land and its legacy, of choosing goodness, of happiness, of devotion to life, of responsibility, of social involvement, and out of that heart which beats with faith in this country and this nation, out of the great depth of pain flowed springs of love. "When the heart is full of faith, it can withstand great challenges. I turned my grief into a new melody. If we go out to meet the diversity, the others, we will know, we will feel, we will see the painful and happy eyes, and even if there is an abyss between us, we can build bridges over them, and all of us in this land are objects of life and objects of peace, and this is the home

K OUR BOYS

#BringBackOurBoys

Banner for three kidnapped Israeli teenagers, 2014.
(*Wikipedia*)

of all of us," she said. Following her speech, Israel's Education Ministry created lesson plans ensuring that her speech and the values it contained was taught in schools throughout the country.

Another prestigious prize and positive outcome impacting thousands of students in Israel resulted from one of the most tragic events in recent years. On June 2, 2014, three Israeli teenagers Eyal Ifrah, Gil-ad Shaer and Naftali Fraenkel were kidnapped by Hamas terrorists as they stood waiting to catch a ride home from their school in Gush Etzion. For 18 days, while Israel's security forces desperately searched for the boys, their families, together with the entire nation and Jewish people worldwide, anxiously waited for information about the teens' fate, hoping and praying for their safe return. Hundreds of thousands of people took to social media to express their reaction to the event. Banners entitled 'Bring Back Our Boys' were placed at intersections and buildings all over Israel and large crowds of teenagers gathered at the location of the kidnapping, lighting candles and putting up pictures of the three youth. Prayer sessions were held in schools, synagogues and community centers countrywide and across the globe. Famous musicians composed songs for the boys and a massive rally was held in Tel Aviv, where thousands called for unity and prayer. Almost three weeks later, the teens' bodies were found buried in a shallow grave near the city of Hebron. A tape recorded emergency call, made by Gil-ad Shaer during the kidnapping and initially ignored by Israeli police, revealed that they had been shot at point blank by the two Palestinian terrorists almost immediately after the kidnapping.

The parents were aware all along that the odds that their sons were still alive were slim but they hung on to the hope that they would see their boys again. At the funeral, Rachael Fraenkel, mother of Naftali, told the crowd, "Each prayer has its own work to do. There is no senseless act of love and charity. A good act stands on its own.

A year following the tragedy, the three boy's families together with then Jerusalem mayor Nir Barkat and Israeli NGO Gesher created the Global Unity Prize – a unique award to recognize and "honor initiatives in Israel and worldwide that are instrumental in advancing mutual respect for others both in times of crisis and in daily life." So far, over two million people have participated in the Global Unity Prize and Unity Day events.

OneFamily was founded in 2001 by the Belzberg family in the wake of the devastating suicide bombing of the Sbarro restaurant, in which 15 people were killed and 130 were wounded. Among the dead were seven children. The attack took place at 2pm, when the restaurant was packed with customers. At the time of the attack, Marc and Chantal Belzberg were preparing to celebrate the bat mitzvah of their daughter, Michal. Stunned by the scale of the attack – the worst of the Second Intifada up to that time – the family made a joint decision to cancel the celebration and use the money to help the victims of the attack instead. They also encouraged friends and family members to send contributions instead of gifts. Within a short time, the family collected $100,000 to help the victims. Since 2001, OneFamily has helped more than 11,000 Israeli victims of terror financially, emotionally and le-

Victims of terror
participate in a
OneFamily event.
(One Family)

gally and the organization has received a number of prestigious awards including the 2011 Presidents Award for Volunteerism. OneFamily has a unique model of working with the victims. It is based on helping develop a family environment for peer-to-peer support. When those who have suffered are connected to others who have undergone similar trauma, gateways for healing are opened and recovery is enhanced. They call the approach "The Power of Together." The key to its success lies in ensuring that no one who has suffered from terror, either as a direct victim or as a family member of a victim, need bear the burden alone. The true healing process begins when the victims believe they are receiving the support they need. Over the years, OneFamily has expanded its mandate from only helping victims financially – often providing essential support that keeps terror victims from falling into a cycle of poverty because of the costs of recovery – to providing support services to deal with the trauma of terror as well. These include group counseling as well as retreats and outings for orphans, bereaved parents, parents of injured children, widows and widowers, young adults, and youth. Social workers at OneFamily are on hand 24/7 to provide support to thousands of victims.

Finally, on a beautiful summer's day in Jerusalem, in July 2009, I was sitting on my balcony listening to music on Galgalatz, one of the main radio stations in Israel, when something happened that I had never experienced before. The show's DJ stopped the music mid-song and made an announcement that anyone living in the southern Israeli city of Sderot along the border with the Gaza Strip, had to run for cover as a terror rocket has been launched

Bomb shelter in Sderot. *(Wikipedia)*

toward their city. Motion-sensors along Israel's fence with Gaza were installed several years ago in order to trigger a "code-red" siren and warn the residents of the city of incoming rockets, giving them approximately 15 seconds to find shelter. It was a surreal moment. Here I was in Jerusalem, on a rather pleasant day, children from a nearby school playing in the street below, while residents of Sderot, only an hour-and-a-half drive away, were running for their lives. At the end of the allocated 15 seconds the radio show host offered words of support and encouragement to its southern listeners and then the music started up again. It was disturbing and before I had time to process the event, it happened again, and then again and in the space of one morning, over 20 terror rockets had been fired toward Sderot. As a follower of one of the biggest international news channels, [preferring to read the news in English,] I kept checking for updates on their website throughout the day to gather more information about what was happening in the south of the country. And yet, to my astonishment, on a day in which over 20 terror attacks had occurred, there was not even one mention of this in the news. I did some additional research on Sderot and I learned that the city and its residents had already experienced over 10,000 rocket attacks since 2001.

I also uncovered the story of Ella Abekasis, a 17-year-old girl from Sderot who, after returning with her younger brother from a youth group meeting in the city, got caught when the "code-red" siren went off. On that dreadful night, there were no bomb shelters, buildings or trees located in close proximity, so Ella took her younger brother, placed him on the floor in the middle of the road and lay down on top of him, protecting him with her entire body. Unfortunately, the rocket landed several meters away from where Ella and her brother lay on the ground and she was hit by shrapnel from the rocket. She died a week later in the hospital, af-ter having saved her brother's life. Ella's father Yonatan said that she had acted like the guardian of her 10-year old brother from the outset of the Qassam rocket attacks on Sderot. She accom-panied him everywhere, slept alongside him, waited outside the bathroom for him and was always with him at the computer on the second floor of the family's home.

Ayala-Chaya (Ella) Abukasis, who was laid to rest in Sderot, was survived by her parents, Yonatan and Sima, her brothers Ran and Tamir, and sister Keren. Thousands attended the fu-neral, where her father read a note she had penned shortly be-fore her death: "Sometimes we tend to forget that life will be over one day, and we don't know when that day will come, and praise is always voiced too late, so in order for that not to happen, I've chosen to tell you [father] what a wonderful person you are. Tell people that you love them and care about them." In July 2011, a large community building called Mishkan Ella (Ella's Sanctuary) was built in Ella's memory in the center of Sderot. The center serves as an educational and social activism hub for youth in the city.

Today, in Israel, there are approximately 880,000 disabled adults and 300,000 children with special needs, approximately 10% of the population, and while they continue to face significant barriers to full integration in society, Israel is constantly moving ahead in its efforts to accommodate and advance the rights of this important segment of our society. In 2012, the Knesset (parliament) voted to ratify the Convention on the Rights of Persons with Disabilities (CRPD), which is an important step in ensuring disability rights in Israel and around the world. And in 2014, an amendment to the law was advanced that provides better accommodation and integration for students with learning disabilities at Israeli universities.

Yoel Sharon was paralyzed in his lower body after an Egyptian tank hit his APC during the Yom Kippur War, an attack which killed 19 Israeli soldiers and left three wounded. In spite of his severe physical limitations, Yoel was determined to continue the course of life he had been taking before the war. He went on to complete his film studies at Tel Aviv University and started what would become a very successful career in the film industry with offices in Hollywood and Tel Aviv. He also got married, had two daughters and lived a very active social life. But something was missing. When Yoel was offered to produce a film about scuba diving around Sharm-El-Sheik featuring ex-commando veterans and the country's top instructors, he listed as one of his conditions that he would only agree to the shoot if he was allowed to dive with the others during the filming. The movie producers agreed and against the wishes of his rehabilitation doctor, who thought he was risking his life, Yoel became the first paralyzed person to learn to dive. He later described the shoot as, "the most exciting three weeks of my life. I had simply discovered the underwater world and as a paraplegic, I discovered the feeling of hovering, weightlessness . . . this incredible pleasure." The experience sowed the seeds for his new life's mission. When the first automated four-wheel-drive jeeps arrived in Israel several years later, Yoel bought one and organized trips for both abled and disabled IDF veterans so they could appreciate the beauty of the country and to enjoy the natural camaraderie that develops along the way. When a good friend of his showed him a device from America that provided paralyzed people the opportunity to ski, he joined a one-legged ski instructor and organized Israel's first snow-skiing course for the disabled in Austria. Yoel described it this way: "Suddenly, I found the ultimate thing – being part of nature as much as one could be at a sports site with everyone else, reaching enormous speeds, passing skiers on your left and right. Truly an amazing experience." Yoel and his friend pitched the idea to the Disabled IDF Veterans Association expecting them to jump on board, but were met with skepticism. They realized that it was up to them to take responsibility for their lives and they went on to found a non-profit organization, the Snow Skiing Foundation for the Disabled. They soon realized that skiing limited their scope of operation; they wanted to include all outdoor sports. So in 1994, Etgarim (Challenges) was formed as an official Israeli nonprofit organization. Yoel explains that Etgarim was actually born during World War II. "I am a second generation Holocaust survivor, a child of survivor parents. My mother is a Holocaust survivor from the Bergen-Belsen concentration camp. My father is a survivor of the work camps in Russia – an amazing story of eight years in

A blind man runs with Etgarim volunteer. *(Etgarim)*

a forced-labor camp near the North Pole – with an escape story that is even more amazing. I think that when you are born to parents like these, even if they don't talk to you about their past, you turn out to be a "survivor" in your genes. I believe that already at Bergen-Belsen or at the work camp by the North Pole, the first seeds of Etgarim were sown." Etgarim aims to empower the special needs population to meet their potential, extend their abilities in all areas of life including outdoor and extreme sports activities and to be a greater part of their communities.

There are many other Israeli organizations that work to improve the life of people with disabilities and special needs in Israel. The following organization stands out – not only due to the high-profile status and character of its founder but also due to the unique care that its beneficiaries receive no matter what the circumstance.

In the summer of 2014, over 4,500 terror rockets rained down on Israel from the Gaza Strip. During the attacks, the town of Ofakim, a small community in the south of the country suffered continued bombardment. The Negev-based rehabilitative village

A disabled person being carried on hike. *(Etgarim)*

ALEH volunteers in Jerusalem. *(ALEH)*

of ALEH, Israel's foremost network of state-of-the-art facilities
for children with severe developmental and intellectual disabilities, bore the brunt of the nonstop fire. ALEH provides over 700
children from around Israel with high-level medical and rehabilitative care in four residential facilities throughout the country.
ALEH Negev-Nahalat Eran was founded by Major. Gen. (Res.)
Doron Almog, one of the most celebrated figures in the history
of the Israel Defense Forces. Almog gained renown for his role as
the first Israeli paratrooper reconnaissance commander to land at
the daring rescue mission in Entebbe in 1976, and later for his participation in Operation Moses. As the head of the IDF's Southern

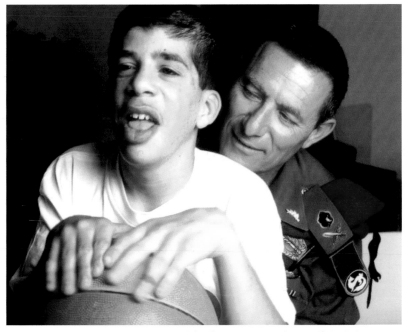

Gen. (Res.) Doron Almog with his late son Eran Almog *z"l. (ALEH)*

Command from 2000-2003, he protected Israel's southern border from infiltration by terrorists from Gaza.

After retiring from the IDF, Almog was motivated by his son,
Eran, who was born with severe autism and developmental de-
lays, to help establish ALEH Negev-Nahalat Eran. Since 2005, the
Negev-based rehabilitation village has provided continuous residential care for more than 200 children with severe physical and
cognitive disabilities as they grow from adolescents into young
adults. In addition to providing services and outpatient care to
thousands of individuals from Israel's southern region, including rehabilitation treatments and therapies, dental care, physio-
therapy, hydrotherapy, and communication and speech therapy,
ALEH Negev also invests heavily in the region, currently em-
ploying close to 300 local residents. Memories of Eran, who lost
his battle with Castleman's disease in 2007 at the age of 23, fuels

Almog to continue his commitment to securing the best possible care for Israel's disabled community.

When the rocket bombardment from Gaza began, residents of Ofakim had just 30 seconds to take cover. Because it was impossible to rush all 133 wheelchair users at ALEH Negev into the bomb shelter every time the siren sounded, the ALEH staff moved all resident into the shelters and equipped them with vital medical equipment and supplies. It was challenging for the staff to preserve an air of calm day after day, making the residents feel secure and comfortable. But it was a testament to their dedication to the children of ALEH.

It's no wonder that ALEH is often referred to as a place where "angels are loved and cared for by angels."

8 One Shared World
Protecting Our Planet

*In the final analysis, our most basic common link is that
we all inhabit this small planet. We all breathe the same
air. We all cherish our children's future. And we are all
mortal.*

John F. Kennedy

Israelis are not just concerned for human life; they
also have a great affinity toward wildlife and the environment
and often go to great lengths to protect both. The World Wildlife
Fund recently ranked the State of Israel as the second highest
clean technology country in the world. Over 83% of Israelis use
solar energy for hot water, the highest percentage in the world;
Israel treats 92% of its wastewater and reuses 75% in agriculture,
and Israel is the only country that entered the 21st century with a

Migrating birds at Hula Valley. *(Wikipedia)*

net gain in the number of trees – even more remarkably in an area that is mainly desert. Over 260 million trees have been planted in the past 50 years. Despite the fact that Israel is one of the smallest countries in the world – only 20,000 square kilometers (8,000 square miles) – the land of Israel has a varied and beautiful landscape with many distinct ecosystems. Israel is blessed with a wide array of biodiversity and is home to some 2,800 species of plants, more than 500 species of birds and 100 species of mammals.

Perhaps one of the most beautiful and unique nature parks in Israel where this wildlife can be seen up close is the Hula Valley in the north of the country. Located along the African-Eurasian flyway and at the junction of three continents, the valley is crossed by migrating birds on a scale unparalleled anywhere else. Studies have shown that roughly 500 million migrating birds made up of

550 species cross this area twice a year, consequently making it one of the most popular bird watching destinations for bird enthusiasts worldwide.

The Society for the Protection of Nature in Israel (SPNI,) Israel's oldest and largest environmental non-profit organization, is behind the success of the Hula Valley. Individuals and families flock to the site every year during the bird-migrating months to catch a glimpse of awe-inspiring sights of hundreds of thousands of birds covering the sky. They also take the opportunity to enjoy the number of nature trails and biking paths in the area and participate in the educational activities made available.

The SPNI was also instrumental in establishing the Jerusalem Bird Observatory in Jerusalem in 1994. Located between the Knesset and Supreme Court buildings, it has a strategic location on the bird migration route between Africa and Eurasia along the Great Rift Valley.

Israeli interest in these birds goes far beyond tourism and many organizations and initiatives besides SPNI are dedicated to protecting the feathered animals and the surrounding environment.

View of the Sea of Galilee in North of Israel. *(Wikipedia)*

Yossi Leshem, known as Israel's "Bird man" and director of the Israel-based International Center for the Study of Bird Migration, has dedicated his life to the study of bird migration patterns. He is a world-renowned expert and has set up a radar system that detects bird migration patterns to avoid crashes that could down Air Force jets. Leshem pioneered the use of mice-eating birds like kestrels and barn owls as a means of pest control.

A national bird banding center was established in Jerusalem and over two hundred birds are banded every day by trained volunteers during the spring and fall migrations.

A wildlife hospital was also founded and serves as the "world's first blood transfusion base for birds," healing many birds injured in flight during the migration.

In a region plagued by war and conflict, it is comforting to know that birds, the symbol of peace, get so much attention.

Another Israeli landmark which testifies to the increased investment and changing attitudes that the government of Israel has toward the protection of the environment can be seen on the outskirts of Tel Aviv. For many years, on the main highway toward Jerusalem, one could not help but notice a massive landfill which sat a mere 200 meters (650 feet) from the road. For most of the 20th century, the majority of Israel's garbage was dumped in this eyesore, which eventually collected more than 25 million tons of waste and became known as Hiriya Mountain or "Excrement Mountain" as locals called it. The sight and smell was horrible, it leached toxic runoff into two streams that ran adjacent to the pile causing damage to the ecosystem and thousands of birds at-

Ariel Sharon Park, Tel Aviv, *Wikipedia*

tracted to the garbage created safety hazards to planes flying to nearby airports. It was also where one of Saddam Hussein's Scud missiles landed during the Gulf War in 1990. In 1998, after the government officially closed the landfill, the first challenge was to contain the waste. The slopes and walls of the mountain were stabilized and reinforced using salvaged concrete debris from construction projects. Then the landfill was capped and covered, and now allows Ayalon Biogas to collect methane produced by the still rotting garbage, which is used to power a textile factory. In 2004, the Israeli government initiated a contest, challenging landscape designers and architects to create a way to rehabilitate the area. The main stipulation of the contest was that the mountain is not flattened or erased in any way and rather used as a central point, allowing the history of the landfill to educate Israelis and visitors from around the world about environmental issues. Israel has now transformed this man-made environmental disaster into a national treasure, known as Ariel Sharon Park. The project is already underway and when complete will include more than 2,000 acres of land surrounding the mountain with ponds, recreation areas, bike and walking trails, wildlife areas, and more, making it the largest park in Israel and one of the principal urban parks in the world. Designed by renowned landscape architect Peter Latz, the west tip of the mountain features a beautiful pergola and scenic vista. This is a key piece of the park and provides visitors the highest vantage point of Tel Aviv and the Mediterranean Sea. Adjacent to the mountain is now a waste processing and biofuel facility. Run by Arrow Bio, part of the Arrow Ecology company, it takes approximately 3,000 tons of household waste or about 1,000 truckloads per day and manages to reuse or recycle 80% of this waste.

Today a robust movement exists in Israel dedicated to the care and protection of animals and strict legislation exists to ensure the proper treatment and protection of animals. The 1994 Animal Protection Law is Israel's main piece of animal welfare legislation. The law prohibits working an unfit animal, working an animal to exhaustion, or poisoning an animal, with a penalty of imprisonment for one year. A 2000 amendment prohibits torture and cruel treatment; inciting one animal against another; organizing a contest between animal; or cutting into the live tissue of an animal for cosmetic purposes. The penalty for offenses in this category is three years imprisonment. This comes as no surprise as Judaism teaches that animals are part of God's creation and should be treated with compassion. Human beings must avoid

Ofir Drori. *(EAGLENetwork)*

causing pain to any living creature and there are also several Bible stories which use kindness to animals as a demonstration of the virtues of certain individuals. The attention that animals get is evidently seen throughout the country but the love that many Israelis show for their furry neighbors can also be felt in other parts of the animal kingdom.

When Israeli photojournalist, Ofir Drori, left for a trip to Africa, following four years in the Israeli army, he never would have imagined that this decision would change his life and that he would become an award-winning wildlife activist, spearheading the fight against the illegal animal trafficking industry in Africa. While travelling to Cameroon, Drori was approached by a wildlife trafficker offering to sell him a young chimpanzee. The baby chimp was sick and abused and it was being treated like a rat. Drori's visit with the police began with asking for bribes and ended with an offer for an additional illegal baby chimp. After telling the men marketing the chimpanzee that he represented an international anti-trafficking NGO, he threatened to lock them in jail for trafficking. They fell for it and gave the chimp to Drori and he named him Future. Researching his experience later on, Drori discovered that in the previous 10 years, there had been few if any incidents in which forest-covered Africa's many wildlife trafficking laws had been enforced. He also uncovered a massive illegal intercontinental ivory trade. According to Drori, corruption ruled African wildlife trade. Since his work began, Drori's organization has been involved in more than 1,400 arrests and prosecutions of major wildlife criminals with one group alone singularly responsible for the killing of 36,000 elephants.

Drori established The Last Great Ape Organization (LAGA) that was later replicated in nine countries forming The EAGLENetwork where Eco Activists for Governance and Law Enforcement led to hundreds of arrests and prosecutions of wildlife criminals. Drori empowers a network of African activists to carry undercover investigations, conduct arrest operations, and implement legal follow up.

In 2016 alone:

- 286 wildlife and forest criminals were arrested in eight countries
- 99 ivory traffickers arrested with the total of 1.5 tons of ivory, including more than 100 tusks and 263 pieces of carved ivory
- 34 great ape traffickers were arrested with three live chimp babies, 68 chimpanzee skulls, 26 gorilla skulls and other body parts
- The former wildlife head and the CITES authority of Guinea who was involved in large scale international wildlife trafficking and corruption for more than 10 years, was arrested
- A large international trader involved in the illegal trade in CITES species such as chimpanzees, manatees and other primates, arrested in Guinea
- A significant international bird trafficker was arrested in Senegal with 111 critically endangered Timneth Parrots and thousands of other endangered birds
- Two ivory traffickers were arrested in Gabon with 206 kilograms (450 pounds) of ivory – the largest amount in Gabonese history.

Drori has won several awards for his work. Prince Philip, the Duke of Edinburgh bestowed on him the World Wildlife Fund conservation medal at Buckingham Palace. At the award ceremony, a WWF official spoke of Drori's accomplishments and told the participants that, "It is thanks to people like Ofir Drori that we still have a hope of keeping vulnerable elephants and other wildlife populations thriving – and keeping a spotlight on the poaching crisis that threatens them. I applaud his bold and impactful work."

Much of what Drori and his team undertake to accomplish involves considerable risk. And although they have very strict security and contingency procedures, incidents do occur occasionally. He admits that, "There are times that I really cannot sleep before we find an activist who has been missing for an hour. With operations in nine countries, that's a huge responsibility for the lives of people."

And indeed, in 2013, he had a near-death experience with a crocodile in Ethiopia. While recovering at a hospital in the coastal Israeli city of Haifa, he met his future wife. He continues to share his model with other activist groups in Africa and around the world and remains optimistic that corruption can be stopped and that the situation can improve worldwide. He has written a book about his experiences entitled "The Last Great Ape: A Journey through Africa and a Fight for the Heart of the Continent."

9 Only In Israel

Israel has its attractions. It's the most dramatic country in the world. Everybody's engaged. Everybody argues. When I leave Israel, I get a little bit bored, you know?

Shimon Peres

"Only in Israel," is a popular saying in the country used by locals and visitors to describe the many bizarre, wonderful, frustrating, humorous and out-of-the-ordinary events which could only take place in a country like Israel. The term has also inspired articles, blog posts, online videos and even a contest, where people create lists and express their own personal versions of "Only in Israel" moments. STATE OF THE HEART already includes such incidences, but the following accounts, truly capture the essence of this term.

Annette and Lior Solomon, two young Israelis scheduled their wedding long before Annette's father suddenly passed away in 2015. The couple's invited guests assumed that Annette would be mourning and that the wedding would be cancelled, so very few of the originally invited guests showed up to celebrate. Facing the empty wedding hall, a relative of the couple, posted the heart-breaking situation on Facebook and to everyone's surprise, 2,000 random people, from all over the country, showed up to celebrate the special occasion.

The year before that, during the 2014 Gaza War, Sean Carmeli, a lone soldier from America serving in the Israeli army was tragically killed along with 13 other soldiers from his unit when their APC was struck by an anti-tank missile. There were concerns that the soldier, who had split his time between Raanana and his home in Texas, would be laid to rest with few family members and friends attending as there was not enough time for his family to fly to Israel. But when word got out that Sean was a fan of the Maccabi Haifa soccer team, fans of the club posted a photo of Carmeli on the team's Facebook page, asking people to attend the service at the military cemetery in Haifa, in the north of Israel. Over 20,000 people arrived to pay their respects.

In November 2016, over 1,000 wildfires raged across Israel destroying 600 homes and over 35,000 acres of land. As a result,
almost 80,000 residents were forced to flee their homes, especially in the northern city of Haifa and areas around Jerusalem.
Experts project that it could take up to 35 years for the forestation
and affected areas to recover. During the three-day ordeal, the
heartwarming response by those unaffected by the fires towards
the needs of their fellow Israelis was overwhelming as hundreds
of individuals, municipal and regional councils, political parties, youth movements and hi-tech companies around the country coordinated their efforts to find living accommodations for
those who were evacuated from their homes. They supplied basic
clothes, food, warm blankets and other household items to families whose homes had burned down leaving them with nothing
but the clothes on their back. While the fires spread, a Facebook
friend, who lives in an area affected by the fires, posted the following account on her Facebook wall: "In our area, the fires were just
over the hill. They were so close that we could feel the heat, cough
from the soot and ash, and hear the sirens . . . a lot. It was all anyone talked about. Some were packing and all that. Many parents
didn't let the kids out to avoid inhaling whatever chemicals may
be in the air. . . . During the height of the action, I went to the local
makolet (convenience store) and stood in line with my items. The
line, as you can imagine, is long. People were buying cleaners of
all sorts because everything was covered in soot. "*Selicha!* Excuse
me!" a guy shouted, "But I must go to the front of the line!" He
was holding a box of toothbrushes and a lot of toothpaste. He said
that he only had a half hour off work, and since there was a lot of

traffic, we had to let him through quickly. Geez! A man wants a bunch of toothbrushes to stock up for the next ten years! Urgent, you know? Well, one lady told him off, "Look! We are all on edge! Did you inhale carbon monoxide or whatever? No? Then stand in line! Here, we have no idea whether we will have a home tonight. Even if we have a house, between the planes and helicopters, and the sirens, and the smoke, who can sleep? And you need toothbrushes?" Turning from him, she said to no one in particular, "I guess everyone goes crazy in different ways!"

I must say that the man was big, very big. If he had wanted to, he could have pushed her (and everyone else) out of line. Instead, he blushed and somehow drooped his shoulders. He softly replied, "I am taking these to the shelter. There are people who only have their purses and a few diapers. Who remembers a toothbrush when you only have five minutes to evacuate? Food, drink, and clothes, they are getting. But no one thinks about toothbrushes, so I thought I'd take a half hour and get some . . . to make lives more bearable. You know?" The line got very quiet and cleared a path for him. As he approached the cashier, the woman who yelled at him came running with all the pacifiers that were on the shelf. "Take!" she commanded. "There are babies, maybe not everyone has pacifiers! I'll pay for them!" Immediately, all the customers abandoned the line and began sweeping items off the shelves – Toothpicks! Lighters! Even cloths to clean glasses! They dropped everything in the man's basket! "Do you have room for more in your car?" One person asked, as people continued bringing miscellaneous things.

Perhaps no other event in recent years in Israel exemplifies the unique sense of empathy and family-like responsibility that Israelis overall show toward each other in times of need, then what took place on June 25, 2006, when Israeli soldier Gilad Shalit was captured by Hamas terrorists who had infiltrated an underground tunnel in a cross border raid near the Kerem Shalom border crossing in Israel. During his five-year captivity, Hamas denied Gilad any contact with his family or the outside world and turned down all requests for contact from the international committee of the Red Cross, in direct violation of International humanitarian law as outlined in the Geneva Convention. The only connection between Shalit and the outside world after his capture and before his release were three letters, an audio tape and a DVD that Israel received in return for releasing 20 female convicted terrorists. Gilad's capture dominated Israeli media for five years and for Israelis it became one of the most important episodes in recent history. During the entire time, Israelis across the spectrum rallied for Gilad's release and highlighted a fundamental principle that in Israel the value of each and every citizen is of singular importance. Israeli journalist Ronen Bergman put it best in his New York Times coverage, when he described the national reaction to Gilad's kidnapping as the inability of Israeli society to tolerate even a single soldier held in captivity. He labeled it as part of "Jewish tradition" to sanctify life and the requirement for each Jew to receive a proper burial. Bergman went on to reference Maimonides, the medieval Jewish philosopher who wrote that there is no greater religious duty than the "redemption of prisoners." The abduction hit home to most Israelis who on a personal level experienced the gut-wrenching anguish that Gilad could very well have been their son, father or husband. As negotiations for his son's fate dragged on, Noam Shalit grew increasingly upset with the government and set-off a national movement to se-

Demonstration in support of Gilad Shalit in Tel Aviv. *(Wikipedia)*

cure Gilad's release. Thousands of demonstrations, prayer events and protests were held countrywide. Advertising and public relations professionals offered their services. The country was flooded with posters, billboards and one marketing idea after another. At one point, Israeli citizens were offered the chance to "write a letter to Gilad" in a font that was made to look like Gilad's own handwriting. Numerous demonstrations were held in the center of Tel Aviv under the slogan "Asking for Gilad's Forgiveness," and on social media networks, hundreds of thousands of Israelis replaced their profile picture with a photograph of Shalit. At one point, a fake "prison cell" was set up in a TV studio, similar to the one in which Gilad was presumed to be held. Local personalities took turns sitting inside it, to feel what it would be like to be in his shoes – all of which was broadcast live.

A children's book Gilad wrote in school when he was eleven years old, was used to show people Gilad's personality. The book was titled, "When the Shark and Fish First Met," and is a Finding Nemo-style tale, about a baby shark who befriends a baby fish in the ocean and against the advice of their parents, they build a long-lasting friendship. According to his teacher, Gilad wrote it as a metaphor for the State of Israel and its Arab neighbors reaching out to each other in peace. In addition to all the other efforts, Gilad's family, together with a dedicated army of volunteers, set up a protest tent outside the Prime Minister's residence in Jerusalem. They sat on plastic chairs day in and day out for five years when they weren't lobbying elsewhere or receiving signed petitions from hundreds of thousands of people. All this to ensure Gilad's release remained at the forefront of the country's agenda.

On October 8, 2011, after five years of isolation and many attempts to negotiate his release, Gilad was finally freed in a prisoner exchange swap for 1,027 convicted Palestinian terrorists. The list of prisoners that gained their freedom included many convicts who had carried out multiple murders of Israeli citizens and others that had been found guilty of attacking Israeli civilians, responsible for a collective total of 569 Israeli deaths. The vast majority of Israelis were in favor of the deal. They stood behind Noam Shalit, Gilad's father, who said there is an "unwritten contract" between the State of Israel and its citizens to secure the release of any soldier held in captivity. A small opposing camp held the opinion that by negotiating with terrorists and giving into their demands, Israel was only encouraging future kidnappings and was thus placing more Israeli lives in danger. Despite their different viewpoints, what emerged strongly from both camps was their sincere concern for saving lives.

On the day Shalit was released, the country held its breath.

Service in banks and restaurants came to a halt as clerks and staff stood watching the live broadcast of Shalit's progress as he was relocated from Gaza to Egypt and then from Egypt to Israel. All over the country, banners and signs were hung welcoming him home. Gilad was everyone's son, everyone's brother. The jubilance of his return overshadowed any negative sentiment that existed as a result of the prisoner exchange that had been arranged in order to bring him home.

Gilad Shalit is a testament to how far Israel is prepared to go to bring back its soldiers alive from the battlefield. There are many more examples that display the lengths to which Israel's leadership is prepared to go to retrieve its soldiers who did not make it back alive from war. On April 2, 2019, a dramatic announcement was made in Israel that the remains of IDF Sergeant Zachary Baumel who went missing in the 1982 Battle of Sultan Yacoub against the Syrian army in Lebanon's Bekaa Valley, had been brought back to Israel for burial at Jerusalem's Mount Herzl military cemetery. Over the course of almost 37 years, the Israeli army searched for Zachary Baumel's remains. In a moving ceremony, attended by the highest echelons of Israel's leadership including the Prime Minister, President, Chief of Staff, Head of the Mossad, Chief Rabbi of the Army, former Prime Ministers and Chiefs of Staff and thousands of Israeli citizens, IDF Sergeant Zachary Baumel was finally granted a proper Jewish burial in Israel. The news was greeted with a sense of national pride at the extent the military was prepared to go for its fallen soldiers. I personally remember as a teenager rallying for the return of Zachary Baumel

IDF Staff Sgt. Zachary Baumel *z"l*

during a youth movement activity and on the night of the funeral found myself standing among Israelis from every walk of life at the military ceremony. Sadly, Yona Baumel, Zachary's father, who dedicated much of his life to finding his son, died in 2009 without learning of Zachary's fate, but the rest of his family, including his mother Miriam in her 80s and his two siblings finally received closure. The details pertaining to the mission to repatriate Baumel's body dubbed "Operation Bittersweet Song" were mostly kept secret as the Israeli army did not want to compromise further operations to bring back the remains of two other IDF soldiers – Tzvi Feldman and Yehuda Katz – who went missing in the same battle. Israel initially announced that a "third country" helped in finding the body and later in the week Russian President Vladimir Putin publicly acknowledged that Russia helped bring back the body. Israeli President Reuven Rivlin eulogized Sergeant Zachary Baumel at the ceremony saying,

Thirty-seven years have passed since then. . . . Thirty-seven years – but today you came home. You came back to our land, our country: to Jerusalem. . . . A young soldier, just 21 years old.

The battle of Sultan Yacoub in the First Lebanon War was one of the toughest the IDF has fought; a battle that left us with an open wound in our hearts. . . . We can say, with full faith, that we do everything – even the inconceivable and the unbelievable – to fulfill our oath: to bring home our soldiers who did not return from battle. . . . Today we can say honestly and humbly to our soldiers past, present and future: We did not give up and we will not give up on this sacred task until all those who fell defending our people and country are brought home. . . . We will not cease until all our boys are back home.

The week before the finals of the Eurovision song contest held in Tel Aviv in May 2019, one unlikely Israeli band got an extended standing ovation at the end of their performance. The Shalva Band made up of musicians with disabilities wowed the crowd and the almost 200 million people worldwide who watched the event with an emotional rendition of the song, "A Million Faces." Following their act thousands of Eurovision fans took to social media to express support for the band and say how the performance had brought them to tears. Many spectators in the audience were crying and the contest organizers called the band inspirational for "inspiring us to think differently about challenges

Shalva band performing at Eurovision, 2019. (*Gabriel Volcovich*)

and acceptance." The two lead singers of the band are blind and were accompanied by a young man with special needs, standing behind them, who used sign language throughout the performance. The Shalva Band were finalists on the local Israeli show "Rising Star," whose winner determines Israel's contestant for the international Eurovision competition. The group quit, however, after learning that they would have to perform rehearsals on the Jewish Sabbath should they advance to the finals. The band's artistic director Shai Ben Shushan told Israeli radio after their Eurovision song that, "The heartwarming response from the audience is so much more important to us than Eurovision." Shalva was founded in 1900 by Malki and Kalman Samuels who created a therapeutic environment in which children with disabilities could grow and thrive. This approach was based on the Samuels' own experience with raising their son Yossi who was left blind, deaf and acutely hyperactive as the result of a faulty vaccination. Yossi's disabilities took their toll on his family. Providing him with constant loving care, they became exhausted and isolated. Many professionals and well-intentioned friends suggested placing Yossi in an institution. Malki refused and vowed to God that if He helped Yossi, she would dedicate herself to helping other children with disabilities and their families. What began as an afternoon program for eight children in a local apartment has grown into a national center serving thousands of people with disabilities from infancy to adulthood from the entire spectrum of Israeli society. Over the course of 28 years, Shalva developed transformative programs to fill needs that were previously neglected. The success of these programs has received government and cultural recognition, inspiring grassroots changes in public policy and social inclusion.

Finally, I recently attended a special prayer and support event organized by good friends in our neighborhood for their 16-year-old boy who was suffering from cancer. At this very emotional gathering, the parents of the boy spoke about the outpouring of support they had received over the years and thanked everyone who was there for their unwavering assistance and encouragement throughout the long and difficult journey. They expressed their appreciation for the countless acts of kindness from friends and absolute strangers they had never met before. The father of the boy said that despite the many unfamiliar faces he could discern amongst the crowd, he was certain that many had been instrumental in contributing support and reassurance in a variety of ways behind the scenes.

He also told the following story: During the week that had just ended, the boy's situation suddenly regressed and he was rushed off to a local hospital in the middle of the night. Upon arriving at the emergency room, he was told by the medical staff that he should be taken immediately to another hospital an hour's drive away as the specialist they needed to see was there at the time. When they reached the second hospital, the boy told his father that he was hungry. The father answered, "Tell me anything you want and I will turn the world upside down to get it for you." The son replied that he wanted chicken soup, which in the words of his father was, "not the easiest item to find at 1:30 am." Not knowing what else to do, the father sent a phone message to a friend back in Jerusalem who said he would see how he could help. Within half-an-hour, two random strangers showed up at the hospital with a "big bowl of chicken soup, rolls, salad, hummus and drinks." The father said that this was one story out of so many others where neighbors, friends, friends of friends, random people, and even doctors had worked together to take their boy into the public domain, where it was as if "he has become everyone's child."

↗ Volunteers collecting vegetables, *Leket Israel*

10 Loving Kindness
Charity in Israel

The measure of a civilization is how it treats its weakest members.   *Mahatma Gandhi*

Israel is a nation born and bred to do *chesed* (good deeds). Its humanitarian spirit knows no boundaries and its efforts focus within its own society, its own people, as well as to nations across the globe. While its ongoing relief assistance to all people is an all-consuming endeavor, Israel's local undertakings are as impressive as their missions abroad.

From emergency response teams, helping the disabled, food collection and distribution programs for the disadvantaged, supporting victims of terror, co-existence and interfaith dialogue initiatives, helping teenagers-at-risk, infertility programs, women's empowerment, human rights, immigrant absorption and so much more – Israeli humanitarian organizations at home operate within almost every sphere of life.

Here is a brief list of just a few amongst the thousands of charitable organizations and initiatives that reflect the caring nature of Israeli society, while highlighting the many issues and challenges that Israel faces from within.

Sayeret Hachesed (SAHI) or "Special Grace Unit" is an Israeli organization that empowers disenfranchised Israeli youth to become anonymous ambassadors for good in their communities. Today SAHI, founded by Oded Weiss and Avraham Hayon in 2009, operates tens of groups around the country, in the areas of Jerusalem, the south and center of Israel. Members of the organization meet once a week to collect food and once a week to distribute it. The activities of SAHI include so much more then food distribution to the needy. Throughout the year they arrange visits to the homes of the elderly on regular days and around the holidays; water distribution on hot summer days and soup distribution on cold winter days; visits to Holocaust survivors in their homes for heart-to-heart talks; house refurbishment and repairs for needy tenants; and creation of accessibility ramps for the handicapped.

Yemin Orde Youth Village, located on 77 acres atop Mount Carmel in northern Israel, is home, school and safe haven to 440 at-risk and immigrant youth from around the world. The Village remains open 24/7, 365 days a year, for youth who have no other place to call home in Israel. Yemin Orde provides a high ratio of staff to students and provides individualized therapeutic care and academic tutoring to those in need of extra supportive services. Additionally, the Village's "Informal Educators" provide mentoring to troubled youth and are available 24 hours a day. The traditions and values of Judaism are woven into every aspect of life at Yemin Orde. Graduates remain connected to the village long after graduation and often return for financial assistance, life-cycle events and celebrations. This sense of safety and lifelong support for graduates is one of the unique elements that makes Yemin Orde Youth Village a model of excellence in Israel.

Leket Israel. With the assistance of more than 55,000 volunteers annually, Leket Israel operates the country's foremost food rescue programs, reclaiming and distributing over half million pounds of nutritious food every week to benefit Israel's poor. Fresh produce, prepared meals, and manufactured perishable goods are rescued or sourced from over 1,000 food suppliers and redistributed free of charge to 195 nonprofit organizations (NPOs) serving over 175,000 needy people on a weekly basis. Leket was founded in 2003 by American native Joseph Gitler. "We are the Start-Up Nation, and yes, we have a flourishing middle class. However, there are still many parts of our society where people struggle every day to put food on their tables for their families. The problem is even more acute in sectors of the country with high unemployment, and with the elderly and Holocaust survivors who live on very small pensions. They desperately need our help," says Gitler.

Krembo Wings is an Israeli organization for children with special needs where each child is "wrapped" personally with love, care, and the belief that they can spread their wings and fly. Krembo Wings was founded in 2002 by Adi Altshuler, then a 16-year-old girl, and Claudia Koby, the mother of Kfir, a three-year-old boy with cerebral palsy after Adi began to volunteer as Kfir's big sister. They currently operate 55 branches across Israel, and welcome more than 1,500 young people with disabilities aged 7–21 from all ethnic, religious and socio-economic backgrounds. Activities are

Volunteers at Krembo Wings. *(Krembo Wings)*

carried out with the assistance of over 3,800 able-bodied youth counselors, aged 14–18, who learn the value of volunteering and leadership. Besides the weekly activities, Krembo Wings operates a summer camp for children with special needs, their families and youth counselors.

In May 2018, the United Nations recognized the important work of "Krembo Wings" in Israel and abroad and chose to grant them the title of "Special Advisor" to the UN (ECOSOC.) Talia Bejerano, the organization's CEO, added that, "The unique international status that the movement received from the United Nations will enable Krembo Wings to raise awareness for the rights of young people with disabilities to live a full and fulfilling social life in Israel and around the world."

Zichron Menachem was founded in 1990 in memory of young Menachem Ehrental, *z"l*, who spent his fifteen childhood years valiantly battling cancer. His parents and loved ones aspired to utilize their shared knowledge and experiences in order to benefit and ease the plight of other cancer-stricken children and their families. Zichron Menachem is a non-profit organization that grants immediate, practical and long-term aid and solutions to young cancer patients from the moment of diagnosis and throughout their battle with illness, as well as physical and emotional support to parents and families throughout the long, excruciating ordeal. Dedicated volunteers, assisted by a talented faculty of art and music professionals, dispense support to young cancer patients in hospitals and private homes from morning until night. Zichron Menachem's recreational centers and libraries are open and accessible to patients and volunteers where applicable.

Simcha LaYeled (Joy to a Child) seeks to help children in Israel overcome illness, injury or disability by enabling them to go on trips, play sports and participate in everyday activities that might otherwise appear too daunting. Simcha LaYeled runs activity centers in hospitals for outpatients undergoing chemotherapy and other treatments to help relieve the parents who are watching them. Simcha LaYeled also provides entertainment and excitement to sick children and their families in hospitals through the use of clowns, magicians and musicians. Family getaway programs and retreats offer children and their families much needed rest and relaxation. Simcha LaYeled also coordinates a motivated group of young volunteers who make all the above activities possible.

Latet is one of Israel's largest Humanitarian Aid NGO organizations. Latet (To Give) was established in order to reduce poverty, for a better and just society, by providing assistance to needy populations, mobilizing Israeli civil society towards mutual responsibility, and leading change in national priorities. The organization was founded in 1996 and serves as a national umbrella organization to 180 local NGO's, assisting 60,000 families all year long. Latet operates with the help of more than 16,000 volunteers around the country who give over 310,000 volunteer hours per year collectively in the various programs operated. Latet provides physical, nutritional, and social aid to over 1000 Holocaust survivors, as well as leadership programming for 2,500 youth, many of whom are at risk, about the benefits of volunteering and social solidarity. Moreover, Latet has published 14 Annual Alternative Poverty Report's which provide a more complex definition of poverty in Israel. Latet continues to remain one of the leading NGO's in the fight to eradicate poverty in Israel.

The Israel Free Loan Association (IFLA) is the largest Jewish interest free loan organization in the world. Since its inception in 1990, IFLA has lent out over $240 million (US) by providing over 54,000 interest-free loans. Conventional charity can often hurt recipients by making them dependent and lowering their esteem. Interest-free loans help without hurting by enabling people to empower themselves as the loans they receive will eventually return. Currently IFLA lends out over $20 million every year to Israelis. IFLA loans help many sectors of Israeli society in numerous ways. They enable Israelis without sufficient means to open small businesses or expand existing ones, help Ethiopian immigrants move out of temporary housing, facilitate student loans to obtain academic degrees, allow ailing Israelis to purchase vital equipment and medicines or undergo operations, assist struggling Israelis get back on their financial feet, and much more.

Mercaz Panim is a non-profit organization which provides emotional and physical support to women and couples facing fertility challenges using a multidisciplinary approach. It combines counseling together with body empowerment and therapeutic massage to enable one undergoing fertility challenges to better cope with the difficult process.

Pantry Packers is the volunteer food packaging and distribution arm of Colel Chabad, the oldest continuously operating network of social services in Israel – established in 1788. Every month Pantry Packers hosts hundreds of volunteers of all ages from around the world in their Jerusalem facility to pack, seal, label and box tens of thousands of bags of rice, beans, peas and other dry goods to be included in the home delivered crates of food and supplies for Israel's poorest families and senior citizens. Families and groups coming to Israel for a vacation or special occasion are welcomed to Pantry Packers and appreciate being able to "give back" to those less fortunate in a fun and meaningful experience enjoyed by all ages. Every recipient of a Colel Chabad/Pantry Packer box of goods is screened and selected on a non-discriminatory basis by the social services departments of local municipalities without regard to gender, ethnic background, or degree of religious observance.

Tzedakah Central/Colel Chabad works closely with municipal governments throughout Israel identifying and screening those in need. The organization also works closely with the Israel Defense Forces both in war and peace distributing army surplus food, and serving as the emergency food distribution system in Northern Israel.

PresenTense Israel, a nationwide and global incubator for tech, business and social entrepreneurs, with ideas to better Israeli society, the Jewish community and world at large. Founded in

2004 by Ahron Horovitz and Ariel Beery, both who have since moved on and founded individual start-up companies, PresenTense, has centers across Israel and in five states in the US, provides these budding entrepreneurs with the skills, knowledge and connections to help turn their passions into reality. A new focus for the organization, led by CEO Guy Spiegelman, who has headed the organization since 2013, focuses on

Volunteers at Pantry
Packers, Jerusalem.
(Pantry Packers)

helping entrepreneurs in the Israeli-Arab and Ultra-Orthodox
communities.

ROI Community, one of the Charles and Lynn Schusterman
Family Foundation's leading programs, is a global network of
activists and change makers from various fields of interest who
share a passion for advancing ideas and partnerships that will

strengthen Jewish communities and improve society. Through its capstone Summit and an innovative suite of ongoing opportunities for professional development, networking and financial support, ROI empowers its members to take an active role in shaping the Jewish future. Today, ROI members are creating new and innovative ways to engage wider audiences in Jewish life globally.

Yad Ezrah Chesed Organization was founded by Reb Asher Freund *zt"l* who was a genuine pioneer of kindness and charity. Before the 1950s, Reb Asher single-handedly saved entire families from hunger and starvation. He was known to collect leftover produce from the *shuk* or market in Jerusalem and discreetly deliver the food to the doors of needy families in the middle of the night. Yad Ezrah was a direct outgrowth of these selfless actions which led to the establishment of Yad Ezrah's multi-faceted charity programs. Yad Ezrah is an umbrella organization providing diversified charity assistance at every stage of life to those under that umbrella. It also serves as a support system for thousands of hard-working families who are unable to meet their monthly obligations due to circumstances beyond their control. Yad Ezrah helps emotionally challenged individuals with their struggles to cope and live normal and productive lives, thereby inspiring them to become exemplary citizens in their communities. Yad Ezrah's volunteers impart to each client a special sense of self-worth and dignity, helping each individual find his or her own strength, regardless of age, religious conviction, or social background. Its programs are designed to encourage those assisted to help others less fortunate, instead of focusing upon their own weakness.

Kishorit is a home for adults with special needs in the Western Galilee, established in 1997 by Yael Shilo and Shuki Levinger, on the land of the abandoned Kibbutz Kishor. Kishorit adopts much of its therapeutic and rehabilitative philosophy from the Israeli kibbutz movement. Life in Kishorit is driven by the principal that, "Each contributes to the community according to his ability and takes from the community according to his need." The members work in the various businesses and service centers in Kishorit and advance communal goals as much as they can. It is a supportive community that provides a continuum of residential, social and vocational services. Kishorit members live full, independent lives, and mature and grow old with dignity. In keeping with its continuum of services approach, Kishorit owns and operates several businesses that employ the Kishorit members, including: a dog kennel where champion schnauzers and dachshunds are bred; a communications center that produces a monthly television show for mainstream Israeli TV; a therapeutic riding stable; an organic vegetable garden; a bakery; a free-range egg farm that sells 500,000 eggs annually; the largest organic goat dairy in Israel which produces 500,000 liters (130,000 gallons) of goat milk; a cheese factory; a vineyard and the unique Kishor winery. The food and fresh produce grown in Kishorit provide for the needs of the Kishorit kitchen and are sold in the general marketplace to generate revenue for the community. Meaningful employment is a critical part of the rehabilitative process and achieving independence. Work provides a daily routine, a place to form social bonds, a way to learn new skills, and a source of self-esteem and self-worth. In consultation with his/her social worker, each member decides where he/she wants to work and is placed in a job that suits his/her strengths and interests.

One of the highlights of the calendar in Israel is **Good Deeds Day** – a day dedicated to volunteering to help the less fortunate in society. The idea was initiated by **Ruach Tova** ("Good Spirit") in 2007. Since that time, the event has been adopted in over 50 countries across the world.

Another popular event is **"Festival Beshekel,"** an annual music festival that allows residents from marginalized communities to enjoy top Israeli bands, with an entrance fee of one shekel (around 25 US cents.)

↗ Israeli kids from all walks of life during
Equalizer Soccer Tournament
(*The Equalizer*)

11 Conclusion
Personal Mission

The little grass-roots people can change this world.
Wangari Maathai, Kenyan political and social activist

Every day in Israel, thousands of interactions take place between people from all different walks of life, each one making a small contribution to the betterment of this country and the world. Israel is in the forefront of international humanitarian efforts despite the energy exerted by some groups to destroy the country and transport this region back into the dark ages. As volunteers for countless Israeli organizations, Israelis fly unhesitatingly to remote locations to help local inhabitants following earthquakes, floods, fires and other natural disasters; medical professionals of all nationalities work closely in Israeli hospitals healing and saving lives; environmentalists offer their advice and services

to African countries for improving air, water and other natural resources; IDF soldiers defend our country by keeping the enemy
at bay; religious leaders create programs of tolerance and co-existence and the poor are kept from starvation with food collec-
tions and donations. Indeed, Israel is continually generating positive results at home and abroad.

In July 2015, I became acquainted with an Israeli non-profit organization, The Equalizer, which recently made headlines when
Prince William, The Duke of Cambridge, visited and interacted
with its members, during The British Royal Family's first official
trip to Israel, in June 2018.

The Equalizer runs special educational soccer tournaments and
clinics throughout the peripheral areas in Israel, teaching values
such as mutual respect, tolerance, co-existence and more. It also
focuses on creating awareness among young people of the importance of education, healthy living and prevention of violence
and racism. Over 3,000 children in 194 schools, participate in
Equalizer soccer clinics, learning activities and training sessions
each year, representing all part of the country and from all backgrounds, religions, ages and genders. You can find boys and girls,
Jews and Arabs, secular and religious, deaf and hearing groups,
Israel natives and new arrivals. It is an extremely diverse and het-
erogeneous project that fosters communication and connection
by instilling the values of sport and tolerance. The participation
of the children in the activities depends solely on their behavior, efforts, presence in school and how it is presented to them.
In case of racism, violence or criminality of any kind, players are
suspended from the team's activities. One of the concepts on the
soccer pitch introduced by Equalizer's founders is the issuing of
"green cards" to players in addition to the yellow and red cards
traditionally used for negative behavior on the pitch. Unlike their
counterparts, the green cards indicate a different type of behav-

ior – that of respect and sportsmanship. If one of the participant's helps another player, whether on his own team or the other, he is rewarded with a green card by the referee. The more good deeds performed by the players, the more green cards they get. At the end, prizes are awarded to players that have accumulated the most green cards.

The green card concept is an appropriate and valuable closure to this inspiring collection of philanthropic and life-saving stories. It reminds us that life is precious and that we all have a unique mission in this world. Almost all the people mentioned in this book had a dream – to make an impact in this world – and as you are reading of their contributions, they are each working hard to fulfill that dream. May we *all* be inspired to dream, and with the proper respect, tolerance and compassion towards each other and ourselves, we can initiate improvements and create communities, societies and a world of well-being, advancement and peace – wherever we may find ourselves! As the sage Hillel said, *"If I am not for myself, who will be for me? But if I am only for myself, who am I? If not now, when?"* (Ethics of the Fathers 1:14).

THE END

Special thanks to the following people who helped make this book happen and all the others that pledged their support to the crowdfunding campaign for State Of The Heart:

Parents-in-law
LORI
and
ALAN LURIE

Parents
LINDA
and
JULES KRAMER

In loving memory of

NEIL GLATT,

from

MARTIN
and MELANIE GLATT,

NICKY *and* JONNY
NEWFIELD *and family*

WALTER
DRIMMER *z"l*,

*May His Memory
Be Blessed*

MONA BERMAN

JOSEF GITTLER,
Founder of
Leket Israel

PABLO KAPLAN,
Founder of
Wheelchairs of Hope

ROI Community of
the Charles and Lynn
Schusterman
Family Foundation

Rabbi
MENACHEM TRAXLER,
Founder of
Pantry Packers

NINA PAUL

YOAV TCHELET

MATHEW FOX

Dedicated in Loving Memory
of
my grandparents and grandparents-in-law:

RICHARD *and* LOIS LURIE;

MOSSIE BERMAN;

HARRY *and* RHONA FALKOFF

and

SIDNEY *and* CHANNAH KRAMER

Notes

Introduction

For a detailed account of the United Nations Durban Conference, from the perspective of a European Jewish student: Joelle Fiss, "The Durban Diaries," AJC. https://tinyurl.com/y2m3gkus.

My organization: NU Campaign: www.nucampaign.org.

https://www.dw.com/en/eu-poll-names-israel-greatest-threat-to-world-peace/a-1022127.

Eleftheriou-Smith Loulla-Mae. "North Korea executes defense chief using anti-aircraft gun for 'falling asleep.'" Independent, May 14, 2015. https://tinyurl.com/yxrlb2sw.

The Peace Index, October 2014. https://tinyurl.com/yyek4zhf.

Alexander Kent, "The 5 happiest countries in the world." MSN, 6 February, 2015. https://tinyurl.com/y53wv9y8.

Gil Hoffman, "Poll: Majority of Israelis support responding to terror with peace talks." Jerusalem Post, November 11, 2014. https://tinyurl.com/y4j32vm8.

David Pollock, "Half Jerusalem's Palestinians Would Prefer Israeli to Palestinian Citizenship." The Washington Institute, August 21, 2015. http://www.washingtoninstitute.org/policy-analysis/view/half-of-jerusalems-palestinians-would-prefer-israeli-to-palestinian-citizen.

List of the more than 32,000 charities in Israel:

Israel Gives website: http://www.israelgives.org/pages/index.

1   "Love Thy Neighbor" – Operation Good Neighbor in Syria

Story of Hillel can be found in the Babylonian Talmud, Shabbat 31a.

The verse "Love your neighbor as yourself," can be found in the book of Vayikra/Leviticus, chapter 19, verse 18.

The verse "You shall not stand [idly] by the blood of your neighbor" – can be found in the book of Vayikra/Leviticus, chapter 19, verse 16.

Syrian Girl Story: I met with Dr. Golender of the Pediatric Heart Department of Hadassah Hospital in July 2018 who related the story of the young Syrian baby and her aunt. Barbara Sofer, Israel Director of Public Relations and Communications for Hadassah also contributed to this story.

Tamara Zieve, "Israelis raise half a million shekels for Syrian children." Jerusalem Post, December 18, 2016. https://m.jpost.com/Middle-East/Israelis -raise-quarter-of-a-million-NIS-for-Syria-children-475716/amp.

Details of Operation Good Neighbor, the Israeli Defense Forces. https:// www.idf.il/en/minisites/operation-good-neighbor/.

Syrian President Assad's Al-Watan Daily Interview, December 7, 2016. https://tinyurl.com/y26glo4g.

Rambam Health Care Campus. https://www.rambam.org.il/EnglishSite/.

I helped arrange several delegations to meet with Syrian patients at Hadassah hospital in Jerusalem in 2018.

The website of Syrian refugee Abboud Dandachi, Thank You Am Yisrael. http://www.thankyouamisrael.com/.

IL4Syria   http://il4syrians.org/

NATAN   http://www.natan-iha.org/blog/

2   Guardian "Angels" – A Global Response

I communicated several times with Israeli mountain climber Nadav Ben Yehuda regarding his story and checked details with several news articles including, Udasen Sharon, "Israeli Everest climber saves Turkish 'brother.'" Jerusalem Post, May 23, 2012.

http://www.jpost.com/Features/In-Thespotlight/Israeli-Everest-climber-sa
ves-Turkish-brother.

Israel Fleet of Love and Hope was included with full permission from David
Saranga, The Huffington Post, on August 22, 2013. David's late father, Eliyahu
Saranga, participated as a junior commander aboard the Israeli warship INS
Misgav (K-30).

I first met Israeli Flying Aid founder Gal Lusky in Tel-Aviv in 2010 and
interviewed her for the final details of the story.

Details of the Israeli Aid delegation to Haiti: http://mfa.gov.il/MFA/ForeignP
olicy/Aid/Pages/Israeli_aid_arrives_Haiti_17-Jan-2010.aspx.

Elizabeth Cohen, "Haiti Day 6 – No one but the Israeli's have come to
help any of our patients that are dying." CNN YouTube, January 18, 2010.
https://m.youtube.com/watch?v=UX-UmrFAWNw.

I was introduced to Dr. Brom directly after the earthquake in Haiti by
Grammy-nominated Reggae singer Matisyahu – we worked together to
support The Herzog Israel Center for the Treatment of Psychotrauma (ICTP)
website, www.traumaweb.org.

I first heard this story from Gal Lusky : Chanan Tigay, "Israelis sneak
into New Orleans to help in post-Katrina chaos." March 10, 2005. http://
www.jpost.com/Jewish-World/Jewish-News/Israelis-sneak-into-New-Orlea
ns-to-help-in-post-Katrina-chaos.

Details of Israel's response to the Boston Marathon was coordinated with
staff at the Israel Trauma Coalition (ITC).

I met with Rabbi Odenheimer several times and interviewed Tevel b'Tzedek
staff for this story.

Details of Israel's global humanitarian missions, Israel Ministry of Foreign
Affairs: http://mfa.gov.il/MFA/ForeignPolicy/Aid/Pages/Israel_humanitarian
_aid.aspx.

3   Light unto Africa – A Vision of Zionism

Yehuda Avner: A Jilted Love Affair in Africa, Jerusalem Post, August, 2006.
http://www.jpost.com/Features/A-jilted-love-affair-in-Africa.

I met Sivan Yaari in 2010 in Jerusalem and my organization ran a marketing campaign with Innovation: Africa for several years. The final details of the story were communicated with Genna Brand, head of communication and marketing of iAfrica.

Mitchell G. Bard, "Cooperation with Africa," Jewish Virtual Library, founded in 1998. http://www.jewishvirtuallibrary.org/jsource/Politics/Africa1.html.

I met with Orna Solomon the head nurse of the Hadassah medical mission to Ethiopia in June 2018 during a tour of the hospital with Israeli-Ethiopian youth. The medical mission to Ethiopia was covered here: "Hadassah Doctors Bring Humanitarian Surgery to Ethiopia," Hadassah Woman's Zionist Organization of America, March 20, 2018. http://www.hadassah.org /news-stories/hadassah-doctors-bring-humanitarian-surgery-to-ethopia .html.

Abigail Klein Leichman, "Top 22 ways Israel helped Africa in the last three years," Israel21c, February 2014. http://www.israel21c.org/top-22-ways-israel -aided-africa-in-last-three-years/.

I visited Save-A-Child's-Heart on several occasions between 2009 and 2018 and NU has facilitated a number of marketing campaigns for SACH. NU Campaign for Save a Child's Heart. http://www.nucampaign.org/campaigns /save-a-childs-heart/.

4   State of the Heart – Life-saving Technology & Innovation

Golan Assaf, News Agencies and Israel Hayom Staff: "Rescuers working to save boys trapped in Thai cave rely on Israeli tech," Israel Hayom, July 3, 2018.

World Economic Forum's Global Competitiveness Report 2016-2017.

I learned the story of Rewalk at the Ourcrowd investor conference in 2017 where I saw the technology up-close. ReWalk website: "Paralysed Claire Lomus Finishes London Marathon." The Telegraph, May 8, 2012. http://rewa lk.com/paralysed-claire-lomas-finishes-london-marathon/.

I met Eli Beer in 2018 and coordinated the story with staff at United Hatzallah.

I interviewed Pablo Kaplan for the story about Wheelchairs for Hope.

By Maya Yarowsky "10 Israeli Companies at the Cutting-Edge of Life-Saving Tech." This article was re-published with permission from NoCamels.com – Israeli Innovation News.

Below is a list of the companies and their websites which are mentioned in the chapter.

Agilite Instant Harness https://agilitegear.com/products/arch-harness-black

Babysense	http://www.hisense.co.il/
HelpAround	http://helparound.co/
Israel rescue	https://israelrescue.org/
Maxtech	http://max-mesh.com/
Mobileye	http://www.mobileye.com/
Nanose	http://breathtecbiomedical.com/technology/na-nose/
ReWalk	http://rewalk.com/
Telesofia	http://www.telesofia.com/
The Emergency Bandage	https://ps-med.com/products/hemorrhage-control/
TOM Global	http://tomglobal.org/
uMoove	http://www.umoove.me/
United Hatzalah	https://israelrescue.org/
WaterSheer Woundclot	http://www.woundclot.com/

5   One Human Tissue – Healthcare without Prejudice

Chabin Michele, "Israeli's quandary: How to aid Gazan's but not Hamas." USA Today, August 11, 2014. http://www.usatoday.com/story/news/world/2014/08/11/israel-gaza-humanitarian-aid/13887853/.

I worked for the International Relations Department of the Hadassah Woman's Zionist Organization in Jerusalem, in 2018, located at Hadassah Hospital. All the stories included about the hospital were from direct contact with the doctors, nurses and staff mentioned in the book.

Marcus Itamar, Ziberdik Nan Jacques, "Official PA daily acknowledges Israeli hospital's medical care for Palestinian children and training of doctors." Palestinian Media Watch, May 22, 2013. https://tinyurl.com/y4re6xkz.

The story of Dr. Shamir helping injured Palestinian was covered by Maariv and other Hebrew press publications.

The story of Ziad Dawiyat and the Braun family appeared throughout Hebrew language media publications.

The story of Haim Attias and Haitham Azloni was covered by Channel 2 News in Israel. I was in direct contact with Azloni through a mutual friend.

Al-Aqsa TV (Hamas), "Hamas: We love death like Israelis love life." Palestinian Media Watch, July 30, 2014. https://tinyurl.com/y4pvz77t.

Israel Defense Force Spokesperson Unit: Tamara Shavit, "180,000 Palestinians treated in Israeli hospitals this year." http://dover.idf.il/IDF/Engl ish/News/today/10/11/2502.html.

Israeli Ministry of Foreign Affairs: http://mfa.gov.il/MFA/ForeignPolicy/Pe ace/Humanitarian/Pages/Israeli-humanitarian-aid-continues-10-Jul-2014 .aspx.

William Booth, "The 'humanitarian aid' aboard a recent flotilla to Gaza fit in two cardboard boxes." The Washington Post, July 1, 2015.

https://www.washingtonpost.com/news/worldviews/wp/2015/07/01/did-the -flotilla-to-gaza-have-humanitarian-aid-aboard-or-not/.

Yoav Zitun, Elior Levy, "Israel seizes activist flotilla headed to Gaza." Ynet, June 29, 2015. https://tinyurl.com/qj3tk6n.

6   Humanity in Arms – A Military Code of Ethics

Website dedicated to Eyal Banin *z"l*, by his family and friends http://www .eyalbanin.com.

The two soldiers' interviews included with full permission from Tower Magazine. Schwartz Yardena, "How Hamas destroys its people through the eyes of Israeli soldiers." Tower Magazine, September 2014.

http://www.thetower.org/article/how-hamas-destroys-its-people-as-seen-thr ough-the-eyes-of-idf-soldiers/.

"Gaza: Hamas's social warfare strategy in action," DemDigest, May 16, 2018. https://www.demdigest.org/gaza-hamass-social-warfare-strategy-action/.

Israeli Foreign Ministry http://mfa.gov.il/MFA/ForeignPolicy/IsraelGaza20 14/Pages/2014-Gaza-Conflict-Factualand-Legal-Aspects.aspx.

Richard Goldstone, "Reconsidering the Goldstone Report on Israel and war crimes." The Washington Post, April 1, 2011. https://tinyurl.com/y5fden8b.

Emily Amrousi, Everyone's hero, Israel Hayom, May 6, 2016. http://www.isra elhayom.com/2016/05/06/everyones-hero/.

Ra'anan Ben Tzur, "Officer tried to save Hadar Goldin by entering smuggling tunnel," Ynet, June 8, 2014. http://www.ynetnews.com/articles/0,7340,L-4555 449,00.html.

7   Turning Tragedy Around

I visited Mishkan Ella on a number of occasions and spoke to Ella's father in 2009. The full story of Ella Abekasis. https://tinyurl.com/y4ub9ak5.

Source of fallen Israeli soldiers and victims of terror: Michael Bachner, "Israel prepares to remember 23,646 fallen soldiers and 3,134 terror victims." Times of Israel. https://www.timesofisrael.com/israel-prepares-to-remember -23646-fallen-soldiers-and-3134-terror-victims/.

I heard Miriam Peretz speak one week before the Israel Prize ceremony at a dedication to fallen Israeli soldiers and policeman in Jerusalem.

I ran the international social media for Global Unity Day in 2016 and 2017.

I visited the headquarters of Etgarim on several occasions and coordinated the story with staff.

I visited Aleh Negev on several occasions and coordinated the story with staff. NU Campaign for Aleh. http://www.nucampaign.org/campaigns/help -a-disabled-child-in-israel-walk-talk-eat-hug-aleh-2/.

8   One Shared World: Protecting Our Planet

SPNI   http://natureisrael.org.

Hula Valley Nature Park   http://www.agamon-hula.co.il/?lang=en_US.

I visited the Hula Valley with my family between 2005–2007.

NU Campaign for protection of migrating birds. http://www.nutees.org/en /shop/Causes/Migrating-Birds.aspx.

I was in direct contact with Drori regarding the story: LAGA Wildlife Law Enforcement. http://www.laga-enforcement.org/Home/tabid/36/language/he -IL/Default.aspx

9   Only in Israel

The story of Annette and Lior's wedding appeared in Hebrew language news publications.

The story of Lone Soldier Sean Carmeli's *z"l* funeral appeared throughout Hebrew language press, including the website of Maccabi Haifa Football Club.

The story is in memory of Raanan Gigi *z"l*, who passed away after an arduous battle with cancer in 2017. May his memory be blessed.

Ronen Bergman, "Gilad Shalit and the rising price of an Israeli life." The New York Times, November 9, 2011. http://www.nytimes.com/2011/11/13/magaz ine/gilad-shalit-and-the-cost-of-an-israeli-life.html.

From 2009–2011, my organization ran a worldwide campaign rallying for Gilad Shalit's release, in coordination with relatives of Gilad.

David Kramer attended the funeral of IDF Staff Sgt. Zachary Baumel *z"l*.

Shalva, www.shalva.org.

10   Loving Kindness – Charity in Israel

My organization NU has run marketing campaigns for most of the organizations mentioned:

1. SAHI   http://www.sahi-israel.org/
2. Yemin Orde   https://www.yeminorde.org/
3. Leket Israel   www.leket.org
4. Krembo Wings   http://www.krembo.org.il/
5. Zichron Menachem   http://www.zichron.org/?lang=en
6. Simcha Layeled   http://www.simchalayeled.org.il/
7. LATET   https://www.latet.org.il/en/
8. IFLA   http://www.israelfreeloan.org.il/en/
9. Mercaz Panim   http://merkazpanim-fertility.org.il/en/

10.	Pantry Packers	http://pantrypackers.org/
11.	Tzedakah Central	https://www.colelchabad.org/
12.	PresenTense Israel	http://presentense.org
13.	ROI Community	https://www.schusterman.org/roicommunity
14.	Yad Ezrah Chesed	https://yadezrah.org.il/
15.	Kishorit	http://kishorit.org.il
16.	Good Deeds Day	http://gdd.goodnet.org/about
17.	Festival Beshekel	http://www.beshekel.org.il/about-en.html

11   Conclusion – Personal Mission

I have met with The Equalizer founder Lior Girassi on several occasions. The Equalizer. http://league.org.il/en/the-project/.

NU Campaign for The Equalizer. http://www.nucampaign.org/campaigns/equalizer/.

Index

About the Author

David Kramer is an educator, author and social entrepreneur. He has spent the past ten years helping Israeli and global non-profit organizations tell their story through a social start-up he founded in Israel. David spends much of his time meeting with tour groups in Israel, connecting them to the reality of life in Israel. He served in the Israeli army and lives in Jerusalem with his wife Tova and their five children.